Public opinion, ideology and state welfare

Radical Social Policy

GENERAL EDITOR

Vic George

*Professor of Social Policy and
Administration and Social Work
University of Kent*

The Radical Social Policy Series provides critical accounts of different aspects of social policy in order to develop the body of knowledge in social policy and administration and to provide a forum for democratic socialist debates in social welfare.

Public opinion, ideology and state welfare

Peter Taylor-Gooby

*Department of Social Policy and
Administration and Social Work
University of Kent*

Routledge & Kegan Paul
London, Boston, Melbourne and Henley

First published in 1985
by Routledge & Kegan Paul plc

14 Leicester Square, London WC2H 7PH, England

9 Park Street, Boston, Mass. 02108, USA

464 St Kilda Road, Melbourne,
Victoria 3004, Australia and

Broadway House, Newtown Road,
Henley on Thames, Oxon RG9 1EN, England

Set in 10 on 11 point Times
by Set Fair Ltd
and printed in Great Britain
by Thetford Press, Thetford, Norfolk

Library of Congress Cataloging in Publication Data

Taylor-Gooby, Peter.
Public opinion, ideology, and state welfare.
(Radical social policy)
Bibliography: p.
Includes index.
1. Public welfare--Great Britain--Public opinion. 2. Welfare state--Public
opinion. 3. Public opinion--Great Britain. 4. Social policy--Great
Britain. 5. Right and left (Political science) I. Title. II. Series.
HV245.T387   1985   361.6'5'0941   84–17881

ISBN 0–7100–9968–1 (pbk.)

To Alice, Gabriel and Joseph

I wish to thank
  Paul Beedle,
    Jonathan Bradshaw,
      Critical Social Policy,
        Jen Dale,
          Pat Evans,
            Vic George,
              Ian Gough,
                Roy Haddon,
                  Sue Lakeman,
                    Ben Marrow,
                      June Matcham, and
                        Two Hundred and Forty residents of
                          the Medway Towns,
who all in various ways influenced the writing of this book. The survey on which much of the argument is based was financed by Economic and Social Research Council grant HR/6629, for which I am also grateful.

Contents

Introduction

Talk of the crisis in the welfare state has become somewhat tedious in recent years. In the early 1970s life was more exciting. A language of crisis, contradiction, conflict, legitimation deficit, state overload or dealignment was the common sense, the small change of social policy studies. The onset of tedium results from developments in the politics of welfare. The apocalyptic theories of fiscal contradiction, legitimation deficit or ungovernability apparently undervalued the elasticity of democratic capitalism. Governments may contain welfare spending and reduce standards in public services without provoking a backlash from the mass that threatens social order. In the UK, recent policies have thrown millions out of work and cut the benefits that the unemployed depend on for survival. Election results show that far from undermining allegiance, such policies may actually generate enthusiastic support.

Discussion of welfare crisis has accordingly moved from the level of grand theory to that of practical politics. The crisis of the welfare state is the consequence for welfare provision of deliberate policies which enhance citizen allegiance, rather than the general social outcome of policies forced on democratic governments which have the effect of eroding the foundations of stability. Such accounts tend to link together three elements: first, the assertion of a sea-change in social policy associated with spending cuts and a change in the form of welfare to expand private market services and focus state provision more finely on the control of deprived minorities; secondly, the linking of the watershed in policy to a

1

reversal in public opinion occurring in the late 1970s; thirdly, the claim that there is a concerted political attack, nourished by the about-turn in the mass attitudes, on the principle of state welfare itself. This account draws on a perception of history as of a decline from the golden age of post-war reform and tells a story of the bleak transition from consensus to conflict, from Butskellism to the new right.

The thesis argued in this book is that this approach is in essentials wrong. There are changes in the welfare state and its economic environment, in the form of class struggle, in the demographic context, in the level of unemployment, in the buoyancy of the economy. There is a real brake on welfare spending. This, however, does not amount to a shift into reverse gear. Similarly, evidence of the welfare backlash in public opinion is exaggerated. In close examination of the story of the welfare state it is the continuities rather than cleavages and conflicts that provide the dominant theme. It is easy to confuse change and difference: the changes that are taking place have deep roots leading back into the original structure of the welfare state and the continuing pattern of popular support for it. This can only be explained adequately through a theory of ideology.

Crisis theory is (in part) a theory about the role played by people's ideas in society. In older versions, demands for welfare spending, an apparent disjunction between cultural norms or expectations of inefficiency from a bloated state and the demands of the disprivileged were the mainspring of social crisis. In the new variant, attitude change is the motor of political attack. The perception of the dominant currents in citizen's ideas as floating free of social structure and thus capable of abrupt change is part and parcel of the world view underlying reformist thinking. This approach poses a radical disjunction between the civil society of family and market and the democratic state: the implication is that a rationally guided interventionism to meet desired ends in the latter arena is a practical proposition because there are no insuperable obstacles to its progress in the former sphere. An alternative approach to political ideas sees people's conceptions of their interests and of the role of a democratic state in meeting them as moulded by an ideology that is to be understood in terms of the basic structures of society. Family and market reach back through ideology to fetter state policy.

From this perspective, the supposed crisis in the welfare state becomes the basis for a crisis in welfare state studies. Facts about the limitations of welfare, the political rhetoric of an attack on welfare and the theoretical challenges of feminists, marxists and the new right are construed as an attack on the central paradigm in social policy as an academic pastime. The argument advanced here is that reformism is ideology generated by the same continuing processes that mould people's perceptions of their interests. This view may be supported empirically. Reformism is remarkably successful in evading the three challenges to it. New policies and programmes to deal with limitations of welfare and the supposed political challenge and to win back errant public opinion are proposed. More important, conflicting theories are redressed in reformist clothing, so that their challenge to the basic model of separation of state and civil society is turned. Reconstituted feminism becomes little more than a critique of existing family and labour market policy, reconstituted marxism a harder-nosed fabianism, reconstituted new-right theory a mixed economy of welfare approach. All the weight of dominant ideology presses everything into a reformist mould.

The principal tenets of new and old crisis theories are set out in chapter 1. Against these, the continuities in popular attitudes to welfare, public policy and the development of the welfare state are analysed in chapters 2, 3 and 4. Chapter 5 discusses the concept of ideology and provides an account of the social foundations of the enduring themes in public opinion. In chapter 6, the notion of ideology is applied to theoretical writing in social policy studies. The elasticity of reformism, despite contradiction by opposing theories, is emphasised.

For supporters of the welfare state the news that the outlook for tomorrow is not radically different from yesterday may be rosy. For those who question how far a patriarchal capitalist welfare practice can advance human interests, the tale may prove less cheering. The enemy is the same dull enemy and the new right is a new distraction from the enduring struggle. The ideology of individualism in interests and of reformism in politics generates the contradictions in mass attitudes that have always been present, and perpetually bridges the precipices in reformist social policy theory. The enemy, of course, is the welfare state in capitalist society itself.

1

Crisis and the welfare state

May you live in exciting times!
> Old Chinese curse, attributed to Confucius

Don't Panic!
> Adams: *The Hitchhiker's Guide to the Galaxy*

The notion of crisis

Aristotle's conception of crisis as the centre of tragedy was of a
sudden reversal or calamity that thrusts a man 'into misery not due
to vice or depravity, but rather to some great error' (1963, ch. 13).
The irony of Oedipus' patricide and incest or of Lear's folly rests
on their conscious actions in a world they know not wisely.
Similarly, social scientific concepts of crisis concern the dilemmas
of institutions incapable of resolving the conflicts that threaten
them and that arise from basic contradictions that are imperfectly
understood.

For students of the welfare state, crisis theory has followed two
quite different paths in recent years. Firstly, a wide range of
traditions assert that the economic contradictions of capitalist
society must inevitably emerge at the political level and frustrate
the policies of the state in welfare as in other fields. Secondly an
approach that has gained favour since the late 1970s reverses the
picture to suggest that political actions in areas such as social
policy can contain and manage the problems that arise from
underlying economic causes. From one viewpoint, demands for
welfare spending and tax-constraint of different kinds from

competing groups and classes are seen as fundamentally incompatible, as a threat to the continued satisfactory handling of the economic system: you can't have the meeting of all legitimate needs and steady growth in a class society. From the other, popular aspirations are manipulated to support a state that cuts welfare, and promises victory over inflation. People can be persuaded to vote for less welfare and more sound money. Politico-economic stability generates crises for the welfare state.

Crisis theory: stage 1 – the crisis in the political economy

The explosion of crisis theory in the early 1970s stood out in stark contrast to the dominant consensus and functionalist approaches of post-war social science. The end of ideology thesis in political science epitomised by Bell's work (1961) and the structural functionalist sociology of Parsons stressed order and stability as the central characteristic of society. The political economy of Keynes showed how this might be achieved by an interventionist capitalist state. For students of social policy, the continued development of the Beveridge blueprint provided the comforting assurance that all interesting questions were closed and that progress was a work of detail. Social policy studies needed plasterers rather than architects.

The crisis theory of this period has been well-rehearsed by many writers (George and Wilding, 1984; Mishra, 1984). Three approaches are of most importance, resting on assertions about class struggle, culture and political interests respectively. All have in common the claim that underlying economic conflicts must eventually emerge within the political level of an interventionist state and stultify the conscious aspirations of policy.

Fiscal crisis and class struggle

An empirical American tradition in political economy opposes the achievements of state policy to those of the private market economy and finds the roots of the resounding contrast between 'private affluence and public squalor' (Galbraith, 1977) in the refusal of citizens to pay taxes for collective services. People prefer to keep their money for themselves. O'Connor and Gough have developed a marxist account of crisis tendencies by linking this observation with an analysis of basic conflicts in the economy.

Marx argued that under capitalism there is a long run dialectic opposition between the process of the development of systems of production which required the ever more intricate co-ordination of the activities of large numbers of people and the fact that the profits that result from this production continue to go to private individuals and institutions. It is argued that this basic contradiction between 'the socialization of production and privatization of appropriation' emerges within the state as government becomes increasingly involved in the market system. O'Connor suggests that the activities of governments can be classified under two headings: 'accumulation' and 'legitimation'. These refer to securing, first, the 'conditions in which profitable capital accumulation is possible' and second, the 'conditions for social harmony' (O'Connor, 1973, p. 6). The problem is that the system of profits ensures that, on the one hand, the demand for state expenditure expands, while, on the other, there is continued opposition to the expansion of state revenues. Developed capitalism requires an ever more sophisticated infrastructure, an increasingly highly trained workforce, more centrally directed capital for risky and expensive projects; and on the other hand more evidence of equality of opportunity, social compensation for diswelfares and evidence of collective care for the needy – all of which are most effectively provided by central government. There is no intrinsic reason why people should be prepared to pay tax revenues necessary to finance these activities. It is not clear that standards in welfare rise in line with its cost, as Hadley and Hatch point out (1981, p. 52). The result is: 'a fiscal crisis, or "structural gap" between state expenditure and state revenues . . . a tendency for state expenditures to increase more rapidly than the means of financing them' (O'Connor, 1973, p. 9).

O'Connor does not develop the implication of his thesis for political legitimacy. However, other writers have continued the argument. Wolfe (1979, ch. 7) suggests that the welfare state may be a passing phase in the development by a ruling class of different themes in the repertoire of democratic capitalism, which will be succeeded by alternative means of social control once it is exhausted. Gough has developed O'Connor's ideas most powerfully in the UK, synthesizing them with Miliband's conception of the state as a battleground for class struggle. He argues that contemporary problems in the British state can be understood in terms of a balance of class forces upon the state, which is under continual pressure to expand; from the working class which demands services but is unwilling to fund them through taxation; and from capital which makes its own demands for the rather different set of services it needs but resists pressures to fund them in a similar way (1979, ch. 7: see also Gough, 1980, p. 9). The point is that the relative defensive strengths of labour (in maintaining real wages against the incursions of taxation) and capital (in passing taxes on to consumers) are evenly matched. It is impossible for the costs of state activity to be loaded decisively in one direction. A perennial stagflation is induced by incompatible demands on the product of the economy. In the long run this may lead to a crisis of legitimacy. 'The welfare state is a product of the contradictory development of capitalist society, and in turn it has generated new contradictions which every day become more apparent' (Gough, 1979, p. 152).

Legitimation crisis and cultural values

A second approach to crisis theory focusses on the capacity of the state to generate sufficient popular support to enable it to carry out necessary functions. Thus the state has a role in aiding capital accumulation as O'Connor suggests; however, the balance of legitimation is not simply the result of the interaction of state policy and the incompatible demands of different classes based ultimately on their location in capitalism. Loyalty is influenced by cultural values which are only partially determined by private property, the dominant capitalist ethic. The state cannot guarantee the cultural values necessary to underpin its policies. This view is associated with the influential work of Habermas.

From an economic point of view, Habermas argues, the state has two main roles: 'on the one hand, the state apparatus regulates the entire economic cycle by means of global planning; on the other it improves the conditions under which capital is exploited' (1976, p. 366). The latter area includes such activities as 'intensifying the system of work (the education system); meeting the social and material costs attendant on private production (unemployment benefit, and welfare state, etc.)'. These activities aid accumulation.

His distinctive contribution is to suggest that in order to carry out these roles, the state is dependent on the cultural level of society for popular allegiance: 'it requires an input of mass loyalty' (1976, p. 375). There is no reason why this can be guaranteed. An example is provided by the multifarious demands on governments for the financing of armaments, space-research, transport systems, occupational training, housing construction, health, education, social insurance and so on. 'The selective raising of taxes, the recognizable scale of priorities according to which they are employed, and the administrative procedure must be such that the need for legitimation . . . is satisfied' (1976, p. 376). The problem is that the social mechanisms that produce allegiance are not under the control of policy, because they originate in a different level of society. That level is only partially determined by capitalist economic relations, so that even success in ensuring growth and distributing more goods to everyone offers no certainty of allegiance. Cultural values of equality and liberty resulting in demands for equality of opportunity, meritocracy and limits on state paternalism may clash with vested interests and the pre-requisites of growth.

The coming of the modern state has swept aside the culture that provided the legitimation system of laissez faire capitalism – the appeal to the hidden hand of the market operating almost like a natural force. Now allocation is more and more the outcome of conscious policy decisions which are by their nature open to challenge. Habermas suggests that one ploy which is increasingly pursued by governments is the attempt to generalise loyalty from the organisation and the impact of particular policies to symbols that represent society as a whole: the appeal to patriotism, to the national interest, the justification of policy as supporting 'the family' in general, even perhaps the rhetoric of the Royal Family evident in recent political discourse, the 'Falklands spirit' and the increasing tendency to stereotype and scapegoat out-groups. The basic problem is that the political system cannot itself guarantee to produce the values required to assure loyalty to its policies. Values derive from culture which is independent of the state, and the cultural system produces motives which may be at variance with what is required to justify the particular planning necessary to contain crisis trends in the economy. Ultimately the possibility of a legitimation crisis stemming from the cultural level of society becomes more and more urgent. This is at root 'a discrepancy between the need for motives which the state, and the occu-pational system announce, on the one hand, and the offer of motivation on the part of the socio-cultural system, on the other' (Habermas, 1976, p. 380).

This approach suggests that it may not simply be considerations of economic interest (put crudely, the fact that more and more taxes are levied to finance welfare that those who see themselves as taxpayers perceive as going to other groups) that threaten the political stability of welfare states. Additional problems arise in ensuring that welfare policies measure up to the values of current popular culture. There is in principle no way of guaranteeing that this is achieved. It remains an empirical question and, for

Habermas, the account of crisis possibilities is phrased in a language of theorems rather than predictions. Legitimation deficit is the ghost ever-present at the banquet made possible by the rational planning of public policy.

Offe's work links economic conflict to political crisis through the production of culture in a similar way. His analysis of West German policy demonstrates the incompatibility between the ethics that link reward to achievement and the requirement to motivate workers in the labour market (1976). The clash between culture and the prerequisites of market capitalism is given an added twist by the intervention of governments in the latter: 'if the capitalist system is not able to survive *without* bourgeois-democratic forms of political power, the contradiction between the economic and legitimation functions of the capitalist state points . . . to the irreversible polarisation of class conflicts . . . to the fact that it cannot live *with* them' (Offe, 1974, p. 54).

This approach combines O'Connor's claim that class conflicts founded in the economic structure pose insuperable problems for policy with the additional claim that a separate cultural level of society can also be the seedbed for demands that the system cannot satisfy. These demands, of course, are not necessarily linked to classes or interest groups.

Indifference, overload and citizen apathy

Both these accounts of crisis draw their inspiration from Marx, stressing class struggle and ideology respectively. A third strand builds on the notion of group rather than class interest and of politics as a clash of rationally based political demands rather than of class forces or of culture.

Brittan argues that representative democracy tends to set in train processes which undermine the conditions of its existence. These processes are:

(a) the generation of excessive expectation,
and
(b) the disruptive effects of the pursuit of group-interest in the market place (1975, p. 129).

The first area has been extensively analysed in a tradition that stretches back to the work of Schumpeter. The central argument of this writer is that democracy is best understood as an entrepreneurial system of government, in which politicians offer policies in order to attract support. Consequently there is a perennial risk of inefficiency since 'democratic government produces legislation and administration as byproducts of the struggle for office' (1961, p. 286). Effective democracy requires a considerable degree of popular self-control. However, there is no in-built mechanism that restrains politicians from making unrealistic offers to the populace in the democratic auction, to achieve power. There is a continual danger of popular disappointment and disaffection, unless a basic consensus to restrain the range of promise in democracy to the politics of the possible is maintained.

The inflation of expectation does not necessarily imply crisis. A strong tradition in public choice economics and in political science has argued that the net result is for government to acquire an unnecessary burden of functions. Tullock, for example, suggests that 'log-rolling' (the process of trade-offs between interest groups) and the services of well-organised special interests will lead to hypertrophy of the state: 'if a given amount of money is to be spent on two different types of government activity, one of which is of general benefit and the other which benefits a series of special interest groups, too much will be spent on the latter' (1959, p. 578). People support their own special interests to a much greater extent than they oppose general taxation for what is in everyone's interests.

Other writers, however, are more cautious. Downs neatly reverses the argument to show that special interests can organise to restrict government budgets to escape taxation with the result that it is equally reasonable to claim that government budgets are overly small (1961, p. 129; 1960). Similar considerations may be applied to the claim that bureaucratic agencies have an inbuilt tendency to expansion or budget maximisation.

Discussion of the implications of excessive expectations for government policy has received further impetus from the work of Hirsch (1977). This distinguishes between popular demands for 'positional' and consumption goods. The central point in an elegantly developed argument is that enjoyment of the latter is proportional to the amount that one consumes, whereas in the case of the former it is the amount that is consumed by *others* that is of the most significance. 'As the level of average consumption rises, an increasing proportion of consumption takes on a social as well as a physical aspect' (1977, p. 2). For example, in an economy where most people walk the joys of car ownership greatly exceed those in one where they are muted by the experience of urban traffic jams. A degree confers more benefits if fewer people have one, and so on. The penetration of positional aspects of consumption into the market introduces a further twist to individual competitiveness. In the long run this leads nowhere, like leap-frog. Similarly welfare state interventions to nourish equality cannot spread satisfaction. Without some new morality to regulate inequality, positional struggle nullifies the benefits of growth and undermines the motivation on which interventionist capitalism depends. People won't work hard if they come to realise that economic growth above a certain level fails to make them better off than their neighbours.

Political scientists have explored similar issues in relation to welfare state 'overload'. Dahrendorf writes 'there are few today who would doubt that modern governments have taken on more than they can cope with, and in doing so have partly responded to and partly generated expectations which were bound to be disappointed' (1980, p. 399). Douglas, in a careful review of the debate, argues that the inability of governments to live up to their promise corrodes allegiance: in the long run 'the absence of popular support must undermine the authority of government and ultimately the authority of Parliament and the whole parliamentary system' (1976, p. 488).

Perhaps the most considered discussion of the overload thesis is provided by Rose and Peters (1978). A summary of relevant issues is contained in R. Rose (1980). The argument questions whether mere expansion in size is in itself a problem: 'big' government may carry out many functions – such as the organisation of transfer payments – with striking efficiency and effectiveness. However, increased complexity may lead to an exponential growth of management agencies: the survival of obsolete programmes; contradictions between the activities of different agencies; and a general alienation of the ordinary citizen from an administrative machine that seems remote and unresponsive to individual interests. It is in this last area that he identifies the most important basis for legitimation problems. Such apathy can support authority in passive compliance. The challenge arises when the state demands positive action. And here, 'indifference cripples authority without causing it to collapse' (R. Rose, 1980, p. 23). The most important action demanded under ordinary circumstances is tax payment. To the extent that individuals seek to avoid this the fiscal roots of the state may be cut away. Rose argues that the presumed growth of the 'black economy' is the most important symptom of any crisis of legitimation of the modern state.

All these three approaches in different ways put forward a social systemic conception of crisis. The interventionist state is undergoing or at least runs the risk of an abrupt and fundamental reversal of its whole direction, because conflicts in areas of society which it cannot control nullify the intentions of policy. Legitimation and accumulation are seen as incompatible and an increasingly uncertain balance on a pivot of limited revenue, because the state cannot control the demands of capital and labour. There is no way that public policy can ensure that measures of government necessary for the economy will be compatible with the cultural values that contribute to citizen allegiance. Conflicting interests pursued by social actors threaten to make the state too large to operate efficiently, so that people withdraw their support. All these crisis-theories imply that state welfare, which contributes both to legitimation and accumulation, forms a major arena in which the cultural demands are fought out and constitutes the bone over which interest groups growl. All stress the role of ideas in the production of crisis – expectations, conceptions of interest, allegiance, culture, indifference, demands, positional aspirations, class-consciousness.

In the late 1970s these approaches have fallen from favour for obvious reasons. Mass support for governments committed to cuts in state welfare indicates that the demand for state spending is not ineluctable. For social policy students, the election of the 1979 Conservative government in the UK and the 1980 Reagan administration in the USA are most significant. However, Gough (1982, p. 45); Wilensky (1976, p. 14) and Golding and Middleton (1982, p. 3) cite the psephology of Australia, New Zealand, Finland, Denmark, France and Sweden in addition as evidence of an international 'new conservatism' or 'new right backlash'. If the long march of the welfare state may be halted, analysis of recent election campaigns suggest that the scope for manipulation of cultural values to retain popular allegiance may not be so limited as Offe and Habermas indicate (Hall, 1979; Golding, 1983). The capacity of governments to defeat organised interest groups and hold down wages also appears to exceed the gloomier prognostications of Douglas and Brittan. The extent to which citizen indifference may be expressed in tax revolt may also be exaggerated by Rose. The recent studies by Macafee (1981), O'Higgins (1981) and Pahl (1984) using different methods show that the black economy is unlikely to exceed 5 per cent of GNP and is not expanding.

The interventionist state caught in the cleft stick of democratic capitalism appears able to twist its way out of the trap. The resilience of human society outpaces that of classical crisis theory.

Crisis theory: stage 2 – the crisis in the welfare state

In social policies studies a fresh variant of crisis theory has
emerged more recently. This is more closely linked to the fine
grain of political events and is empirical rather than theoretical in
outlook. Again the central theme is the failure of a social
institution to achieve its goals due to the operations of forces
beyond its control. Again the role of ideas is stressed. Now,
however, the institution in question is the welfare state rather than
the capitalist state. The ideas are popular antagonism to welfare
rather than demands for more spending. The order of crisis
argument is reversed, to put democracy back in the driving seat.
Rather than the frustration of state planning by the excrescence of
economic contradictions at the political level, the claim is that a
popularly supported retrenchment of policy is part of the process
that enables the political system to handle economic conflicts. The
crisis for the welfare state is a solution rather than a symptom of
crisis elsewhere.

This theory has three main elements, interwoven about the
central fact of the decline of the British economy. Britain's
economic malaise is discussed extensively elsewhere (for example,
Gough, 1979; Prest and Coppock, 1982, pp. 52–4). The economic
growth rate of every OECD member state has exceeded that of
Britain over the period since the Second World War. The long-run
problem of slow growth and consequent decline as a world power
was compounded by the effect of the 1973 energy crisis. The
British GDP did not return to the 1973 level until 1978 (Gough,
1979, p. 132). Those who study the crisis in the welfare state are
concerned with the political response to economic difficulties. The
three factors in explanation are, first, the assertion of a sea-change
in public opinion marking a decisive shift against the welfare state
and occurring in the early or mid-1970s. This is situated by the
second factor, an account of the post-war development of the
welfare state as a journey from political consensus on welfare aims
to the conflict marked by sudden unpopularity. The third factor is
the identification of a contemporary reversal in public policy,
reflecting the ideological about-turn. This makes possible a
restructuring of the welfare state, a new departure in its history
that strikes a new balance in the conflicting forces that led to
economic difficulties. The claim in a nutshell is that the new right
has orchestrated a reversal in popular support for welfare riding on
a longer term transition from consensus to conflict in the political
climate of the welfare state era.

Public opinion

Golding and Middleton's influential study of welfare imagery summarises the main themes in this area:

> The argument . . . in outline is as follows . . . The early promise of the welfare state has not been fulfilled . . . the failure of the welfare state is common ground across the political spectrum. Of the available diagnoses, those that emphasise the damaging burden of welfare expenditure and the abuse of social security . . . have received privileged authority . . . Economic crisis has liberated a full-scale assault on the welfare consensus, which was in fact never very firmly attached to popular consciousness (1982, p. 205).

The public burden view of the welfare state is supported by the political economy of Bacon and Eltis which argues that the state sector in the UK pre-empts scarce resources (particularly personnel) that could be used more profitably elsewhere (1976). Further evidence for the view that most people see the welfare state as a burden rather than a direct benefit to themselves is provided in Alt's analysis of British Election Studies from the mid-1960s to 1974. 'On questions of spending on social services people are supporting . . . a benefit which will largely go to others.' There is 'a tendency . . . for economic stress to be associated with less generosity . . . favouring . . . spending cuts over taxation' (1979, p. 258). The view that the overwhelming popular attitude is of suspicion of a welfare state that funnels hard-earned money to the undeserving is echoed by Donnison (1979, p. 155); Klein (1980a, p. 26); Glennerster (1983, p. 8); MacGregor (1981, ch. 5); Bosanquet (1983, p. 1) and others. Rose and Rose argue 'in the face of a powerful ideological attack mounted by the new right . . . the very idea of collective welfare itself is at stake' (1982, p. 18). The thesis of a general welfare backlash in a period of economic constraint is pointed by the particular issue of the rise of public concern at social security abuse. Golding and Middleton see a specific attack on the needy minority of claimants as the focus of generalised dissatisfaction with state welfare: 'The crisis in the British economy has become the occasion for a social derision of the poor so punitive as to threaten the very props of the welfare state' (1982, p. 5). This is again echoed in MacGregor's assertion that 'at present the poor are under attack' (1981, p. 180), in Deacon's analysis of the 'scrounger phobia' of the mid-1970s (1977, 1978) and in the work of writers mentioned above. Sarlvik and Crewe demonstrate that the proportion of respondents to British Election Study questionnaires agreeing that social welfare benefits 'had gone too far' has 'increased significantly' between 1970 and 1979 (1983, p. 172).

The twin themes of public burden and contempt of the undeserving needy have as their obverse support for the privatisation of public services. Harris and Seldon have put the case for a shift in public opinion in this direction in the welfare arena most forcibly (1979). In a series of surveys from the early 1960s they chart an increase in popular support for the dismantling of the system of tax-financed universal health care and mass education, and the substitution of voucher, subsidised and private insurance systems.

The politics of the welfare state era

The thesis that popular support for the welfare state in general and social welfare for the poor in particular collapsed at some time in the 1970s is buttressed by the second major theme of the new crisis theory: a particular reading of post-war history.

A large number of writers from many theoretical standpoints interpret the period since the 1940s as a journey from consensus to conflict, from Butskellism to the new right, almost a decline and fall from the Golden Age of Community, Fraternity, Equality and Beveridge. Gough writes 'ideologically, Thatcherism marks a shift from the consensus politics, which have characterised post-war British governments, both Labour and Tory' (1982, p. 50). Seldon analyses the new policies of the 1979 Conservative Government: 'politicians have caught up with public opinion that was . . . increasingly reflecting market forces' (1981, p. 47). Abel-Smith (1983), Bosanquet (1983), Hadley and Hatch (1981) and many others identify the central features of the development of public opinion and of state policy as a transition from welfare state consensus through the sea-change of the 1970s to the backlash of the present.

From the perspective of defenders of the welfare state, the approach contains an element of Manicheanism, of the eschatology of life as a struggle between forces of light and darkness which no side can permanently win. The current ascendancy of the forces of evil is explained in various demonologies. MacGregor (1981), Field (1981), Le Grand (1982) and Abel-Smith (1983) point to the failure of the Labour Party to mobilise support for an unequivocal defence of welfare. Golding and Middleton (1982) argue the influence and vested interests of the commercial media. Hall places the emphasis on the new right itself, and its capacity to mobilise particular strands in popular ideas (1979). Gough stresses economic weakness (1979), Alt the vulnerability of a popular conception of welfare as a system that channels resources to others (1979). Other writers discuss the limitations of professional and bureaucratic administrations in meeting popular interests (Hadley and Hatch, 1981; Wilding, 1982) or point to a generalised paternalism (Weale, 1983). Yet others stress the changes in conception of self-interest produced by the development of the welfare state itself (Dunleavy, 1981; Duke and Edgell, 1983). Rose and Rose emphasise the everyday life experience of the welfare state (1982). Whatever the nature of the demon involved in particular analyses its role is the same: to explain how a presumed consensus of political support for state welfare in the 1950s turned into a mass attack on a beleaguered social policy in the 1980s.

The sea-change in policy

The third facet of contemporary crisis theory builds on the account of new directions in public opinion to produce an analysis of the new directions in state policy consonant with it. Here, there are three main issues. First, the cuts. A rhetoric of expenditure constraint has been the backdrop to the politics of both major parties since Crosland announced to local authorities in 1975 that 'the party was over' and Callaghan assured the 1976 Labour Party Conference: 'we used to think we could spend our way out of recession . . . that option no longer exists.' As Gough (1979) points out, the policies of recent Conservative governments represent 'more (or rather less) of the same' with restraint biting most bitterly on housing and education budgets.

The second new direction of policy is the extension of the market through the denationalisation of state enterprises. 'We have done more to roll back the frontiers of socialism than any previous government,' the prime minister declared in her keynote speech to the 1982 Conservative Party Conference. The main policy directions in the welfare area concern the sale of council housing, the encouragement of private landlordism, legislation to make occupational sick pay provision compulsory and new subsidies to private schooling and health care. These have not so far radically altered the make-up of the welfare state. Privatisation

17

has gone further in industrial policy. By 1983 a range of enterprises including Cable and Wireless, Associated British Ports, Britoil, the National Freight Corporation, and parts of British Aerospace had been sold off. The 1983 manifesto set out plans to denational-ise British Telecom, Rolls Royce, British Airways, British Steel, British Airports, British Shipbuilders, the National Bus Company and British Leyland. It is unclear how feasible these proposals are.

The third issue concerns a reversal of the limited gains made by women in welfare policies since the mid 1960s. Maternity pay legislation has been weakened and the Family Policy Group put forward proposals to the Cabinet in 1983 to reorganise welfare benefits to encourage women to stay in the home. The rise in unemployment and cuts in the state sector have penalised women workers. Restrictions in spending, together with the extension of community care schemes, result in a greater burden being borne by women caring for dependants in the home.

Underlying all these particular policy directions is the sudden rise in unemployment, from under 3 per cent in 1974 to over 14 per cent by 1983. This development weakens working-class resistance to cuts and the expansion of private services. It is also responsible for most of the increase in the numbers in poverty. Burghes, in an analysis of the most recent available official statistics, shows that the numbers living below supplementary benefit level had risen dramatically by 24 per cent between 1979 and 1981. This is the sharpest rise in poverty since the estimates of Abel-Smith and Townsend in the mid-1960s. Most of the new poor are unemployed (Burghes, *New Society* 3/11/83, p. 211). Opinion differs as to the extent of which unemployment is the result of government economic policy. It is clear that the framework of misery for the minority is an important factor in any assessment of the develop-ments in social welfare in the late 1970s.

Many writers see current changes as piecemeal developments (for example, O'Higgins, 1983). However, two comprehensive interpretations exist. These understand new directions in welfare in terms of the fundamental social cleavages of class and gender. First, Gough (1979, 1982) analyses the changes as an attempt to 'restructure' the welfare state, and achieve a decisive shift in the balance of class forces. Cuts in welfare benefits to strikers, and the refusal of government to tackle unemployment, go hand in hand with new trade union legislation and the divisive effects of encouragement of house ownership, the spread of privatisation and the undermining of universalism to weaken the working class. This position is echoed by Leonard (1979); Corrigan (1979); Hall et al. (1978) and Harrison (1979). A second perspective stresses gender rather than class politics. The target of restructuring is women rather than the working class and the objective is the maintenance of the system of dependence in the family.

> Political and ideological processes carry considerable weight in the construction of women's oppression and should be attacked . . . In the present situation . . . public sector cuts are likely to increase women's dependence on men (Barrett, 1980, p. 264).

The implications of the state's contraction for the exploitation of women as carers are traced out by several writers (Finch and Groves, 1980; Oakley, 1981; Sayers, 1982, p. 168; Lewis, 1983, p. 120; Ungerson, 1982).

The significance of policy changes lies in their relation to the themes of earlier crisis theory. If government can successfully withdraw from the welfare aspects of its legitimation function, can shrug off responsibility for redistributing social resources according to cultural values, can present a contracted aspect to the citizenry, the crisis tendencies discussed above may be contained. A restructured welfare state may achieve a new balance of forces of class or interest groups which ensures the stability of capitalism.

The new direction in crisis theory

The new crisis theory contains the principal themes of an abrupt reversal shattering a previous order and of the incapacity of the order to turn the threat by its own conscious activity – to plan against disaster – of the earlier conceptions. It also stresses the centrality of the role of ideas, in this case as the grist for political change. The difference lies in the more precise focus of the new theories. What is at stake is not allegiance to the state or political order in general, but the maintenance of state responsibility for large-scale social services in the areas defined after the Second World War. State interventionist capitalism can weather large-scale crises provided that it is allowed to re-write some of the rules of the game. From this viewpoint, the welfare state becomes simply a passing phase, a particular equilibrium struck in the constant struggle to achieve a balance of class forces as Wolfe (1979) suggests.

Earlier writers who discussed the crisis in the interventionist state, emphasised the inability of capitalist governments to resolve the balance of pressures on them, turn which way they might. The central point of the new approach is that specific policies, attacking state welfare, enable governments to satisfy the demands of ideology and capitalism and to maintain stability. The reversal in public opinion puts the state back in command. If popular suspicion of welfare enables large-scale cuts in spending and support for private provision, the conflict, identified by O'Connor, between support for capital accumulation and legitimation functions may be resolved. Similarly, the cultural shifts implied may allow the state to retreat from the assumption of responsibility for welfare that, Habermas argues, forces it inevitably to risk the loss of popular allegiance. The excessive expectations of policy which produce citizen indifference may be minimised. The sea-change of the 1970s, so far as the welfare state goes, renders crisis-tendencies manageable.

The thesis of this book is that an imminent crisis in the welfare state as a response to public opinion and a watershed in the politics of welfare is mistaken. This is not to deny the importance of economic decline, nor its significance for social policy. This is part of a whole range of issues affecting welfare, and is to be analysed alongside changes in demography, levels of living, work and family patterns in its influence on policy. Most of these factors are long-run. The point of the argument is that the political conflicts that threaten the welfare state now have been inherent in its structure since its inception. The impact of abrupt reversal in welfare policy or popular opinion is exaggerated. The real enemy of those who seek to advance welfare is not a sudden confrontation, but the continuing development of overall contradictions and ambiguities in the welfare state: the old enemy, not the new right.

2

Public opinion and welfare issues

'A plague of opinion! A man may wear it on both sides, like a leather jerkin'

William Shakespeare, *Troilus and Cressida*

'Of course we welcome the growth of private health insurance. There's no contradiction between that and supporting the NHS'

Margaret Thatcher, 1982

This chapter has two tasks. The first is to present a picture of public attitudes to the welfare state in the three areas identified as central themes in social policy by the new crisis theory: a shift against the public provision of welfare, support for privatisation and reversal of the gains made by women. The evidence discussed comes mainly from opinion surveys and centres on discussion of a study of these issues carried out in the Medway area in 1981. This study covers the widest range of aspects of public and private welfare issues of any survey to date. Further details are given in Taylor-Gooby (1982). The evidence does not support the claim that people have turned against the welfare state.

The second task is to explain how this view of public opinion appears sufficiently plausible to gain overall acceptance, if it is misleading. The evidence used to reinforce it will be reviewed and reinterpreted in consideration of each of the three aspects of opinion.

Problems of opinion survey

A number of points should be made about the shortcomings of attitude survey data before the analysis is presented. Firstly, what people say about their opinions is a poor guide to their likely actions and vice versa. Fishbein and his colleagues point out that attitudes and subjective norms may influence behavioural intentions, but 'further variables may intervene between intentions and overt behaviour' (Fishbein, Thomas and Jaccard, 1976, p. 8). Conversely, Davies shows that the strength of feelings of stigma may not be inferred from whether people choose to claim free school meals or not because of the countervailing significance of a free source of food for children in the budgets of poor families (1978, pp. 126–9). Secondly, it is well known that attitude structures, as revealed by survey, show considerable instability over time. Thus when Converse re-interviewed a sample of respondents to a survey of attitudes to American Government Policy after a lapse of four years, he found that 65 per cent of individuals had changed their minds, although the overall pattern of opinions had changed little. Similar individual volatility within a structure of overall stability is reported in the UK (Butler and Stokes, 1971, ch. 8; Kavanagh, 1983, p. 14). Thirdly, information is collected from individuals usually through a process of one-off conversations with middle-class strangers on topics that may not be of much interest to the person questioned. On the one hand, the data gathered by this process may be influenced by circumstantial factors (courtesy, obstinacy, the desire to conform, feelings about the interview situation); on the other, as Bourdieu points out, the method is inherently individual and obscures recognition of the fact that political action in a mass society is collective (Mattelard (ed.), 1979). Finally, many agencies, and most importantly governments, devote considerable efforts to influencing opinion on political issues by the manipulation of information flow, persuasive communication and so on (Judge and Hampson, 1980). These factors mean that attitude data is propaganda biased, individualist, situational, volatile and no guide to behaviour. However, simply taken as an indication of the state of play of opinions in the minds of the public, which may or may not be influenced by government itself, it may be useful. In relation to new crisis theory, no assertions about the likelihood of popular action (or inaction) other than political support are involved, unlike earlier theories, which stressed tax revolt or the withdrawal of allegiance. Opinion surveys provide an account of the general structure of political ideas that is difficult to obtain from any other source. Provided the evidence is interpreted with care it may help in assessing issues about the contribution of changes in public ideas to public policy.

The shift against the welfare state

Two recent attitude studies support the view that there has been a move in opinion against public welfare provision. Golding and Middleton locate the change in the mid 1970s. Alt's re-analysis of British Election Survey data puts it somewhat earlier. In addition, a number of other surveys including the 1976 Eurobarometer study of perceptions of poverty and surveys carried out for the review of supplementary benefits by the Schlackman Organisation (1978) may be cited to support the thesis.

Golding and Middleton's account claims that state welfare is perceived as a public burden:

> Generally it seems there is considerable suspicion of additional public expenditure on social security and welfare among groups who feel they have more to lose as taxpayers, than to gain as beneficiaries. This fairly uniform response may reflect the increasingly orthodox belief that personal taxation has become too high, attached to the related view that rising taxation is a burden imposed by excessive public expenditure notably in the field of social services and social security (1978, pp. 93–4).

Alt asserts that 'on questions of spending on social services, people are supporting an idea which is altruistic: they are supporting a benefit which will largely go to others' (1979, p. 272). In fact, public policy does not impose a burden on the mass of the population through redistribution to the poor. It is increasingly recognised that most of the money spent by government on social welfare goes to the better off. A recent authoritative study concludes:

> almost all public expenditure on the social services in Britain benefits the better off to a greater extent than the poor. This is not only true for services such as roads where, due to the insignificant role played by a concern for equality in determining policy, such an outcome might be expected; it is also true for services whose aims are at least in part egalitarian, such as the National Health Service, higher education, public transport and

the aggregate complex of housing policies (Le Grand, 1982, pp. 1–2; see also Titmuss, 1955; Sinfield, 1978; Field, 1981; Hadley and Hatch, 1981; Nicholson, 1974).

Of course, the general public may not recognise this fact and thus bite the hand that feeds them.

Many writers assert that the pattern of ideology is such that subsidies to the worst off bulk large in popular imagination, while those to middle and higher groups are largely ignored. The most sophisticated version of this approach is developed by Dunleavy, in his discussion of consumption sectors. 'Sectors are lines of vertical division in a society, such that certain common interests are shared between social classes in the same sector, while within a social class, sectoral differences reflect a measure of conflict of interests' (1979, p. 420). Dunleavy demonstrates that in the case of two important urban consumption processes – transport and housing – there is a high degree of overlap within both state provided and market sectors. Owner-occupation is highly corre-lated with car ownership, council tenure to reliance on public transport. The point is that 'when the two locations are considered *together* it is apparent that involvement in wholly individualised or wholly collective modes of housing and transport consumption varies across social grades much more markedly than the involve-ment in each type of location alone' (1979, p. 425). The state/private distinction in consumption is cumulative not chaotic, and the interests generated by the involvement of the state in provision of services may therefore reinforce each other across class boundaries.

Of course, state subsidies flow to both state and market divisions of each sector: Le Grand concludes his analysis of the impact of tax exemptions and direct subsidies for housing by pointing to 'substantial inequalities of public expenditure with owner-occupiers receiving more than private or public tenants and the better off receiving more than the less well off' (1982, p. 100). Similar conclusions apply to transport (ch. 6). Dunleavy's point is that popular ideology, which influences political discourse, paints a different picture: 'the end result of these perceptions is a basically inaccurate picture of home-owners as paying their own way and of council tenants as heavily subsidized, and non-rate paying' (1979, p. 430), and comparable attitudes apply to transport. The dominant ideology influences party programmes and interests in consumption sector affect voting behaviour. Dunleavy is able to demonstrate that home ownership and car ownership influence political alignment in addition to occupational class and age in analysis of Gallup poll data at the time of the 1974 election. Similar results are reported by Duke and Edgell in a survey of perceptions of welfare cuts in Manchester (1981).

The assertion that welfare as a whole is denigrated because it is seen by many as a public burden that can be less easily borne in a time of expenditure constraint is thus implicitly a claim about ideology understood as a counter-factual pattern of beliefs. People think state subsidies flow from consumers in the private sector to a minority in the public sector and this pattern is repeated with re-doubled force in relation to the most obvious and needy minority of consumers – state beneficiaries.

Le Grand's work focusses on welfare in kind. The most important aspect of the welfare state omitted is the income transfer programme of the social security system. Analyses of this area show that cash benefits do distribute to the poor and the most needy (if this is understood as larger households). This is particularly true of means-tested benefits such as Supplementary Benefit and Family Income Supplement and Unemployment and Sick Benefits (Nicholson, 1974, pp. 77–8). This picture is moderated somewhat if attention is paid to the shortcomings of the data on which it is based (Field, 1981; Nicholson and Brittan, 1979, p. 325; Nissel, 1978, p. 4), and the impact of occupational welfare which is subsidised through tax reliefs and tends to benefit the better off is taken into account (Pond in Walker (ed.), 1982). However, it does seem plausible to regard state social security as the most redistributive area of state welfare. It is significant that much of Golding's study is focussed on this area.

In Golding and Middleton's content analysis of the media treatment of welfare which identifies the issue of central relevance to the survey, the topic-area is defined as 'the responsibilities of the Secretary of State for Social Services' (1982, p. 68). This is interpreted narrowly, so that the whole field of health care is omitted. In analysis of survey data, public concern at abuse by able-bodied unemployed scroungers is emphasised. However, evidence of strong support for the elderly and the sick is not given equal prominence. 'When asked who they think most deserve to get money from the welfare state, people again nominate the old and sick' (p. 169). When people were asked to describe who they had in mind when thinking of the poor 'it was the old who were most frequently mentioned' (p. 189). Retirement pensions are the biggest single item in the social security budget, accounting for about three quarters of total expenditure (Judge, 1981, p. 453). Because they apply, ultimately, to the mass of the population they are less likely to be understood as 'altruistic' redistribution to others. The study provides a partial picture of attitudes to state welfare, and one most likely to bring out concern at the burden of spending.

A similar picture emerges in the British Election Survey data (Table 1). Variations in question design mean that it is only possible to present a general outline of patterns in opinion about welfare policy over the period from the early 1960s to the late 1970s. There does seem to have been a general decline in support

TABLE 1
Attitudes to welfare spending: the evidence of British election studies (%)

(a) *The earlier studies*
If the government had a choice between reducing taxes and spending more on the social services, which should it do?

	1963	1966	1969	1970
Tax cuts	52	55	69	65
Social services increase	41	36	21	27
Don't know	7	9	10	8
Number	2009	1877	1114	1845

Do you feel the government should spend more on pensions and social services, or do you feel that spending on social services should stay about as it is now?

	1964	1966	1969	1970
More	77	55	43	56
As now	20	41	44	36
Less	(not asked)		8	4
Don't know	3	4	5	4
Number	1969	1877	1114	757

Source: Butler and Stokes, 1974, p. 459.

(b) *The later studies*

		Feb 1974	Oct 1974	1979
Social services	Social services and benefits have gone too far and should be cut back a lot	11	13	20
	Cut back a bit	22	25	29

Social services	Social services and benefits should stay much as they are	35	32	26
	More social services and benefits are needed	32	27	20
	Have gone much too far	n/a	12	21
	A little too far	n/a	22	29
Welfare benefits	Are about right	n/a	42	33
	Have not gone quite far enough	n/a	18	13
	Not gone nearly far enough	n/a	6	4
	Very important that more money be put into the NHS	n/a	47	52
	Fairly important	n/a	37	35
The NHS	Doesn't matter	n/a	8	6
	Fairly important that more money should not be put into the NHS	n/a	6	5
	Very important	n/a	2	2
	Very important that more money be put into getting rid of poverty	n/a	50	46
	Fairly important	n/a	34	34
Poverty	Doesn't matter	n/a	9	12
	Fairly important that more money should not be put into getting rid of poverty	n/a	4	6
	Very important	n/a	2	2
	Very important that income and wealth be redistributed in favour of ordinary people	n/a	23	25
	Fairly important	n/a	31	27
Redistribution	Doesn't matter	n/a	19	22
	Fairly important that income and wealth should not be redistributed in favour of ordinary people	n/a	17	16
	Very important	n/a	10	10
	Number:	2431	2284	1871

Source: Sarlvik and Crewe, 1983, pp. 169, 170, 191, 193; Sarlvik and Crewe, 1974, p. 280.

27

for state spending as against tax cuts through the period. However further questions asked in the 1970s make it possible to examine the level of support for particular areas of state spending. It can be seen that while welfare benefits are unpopular, the NHS, anti-poverty programmes and the redistribution of wealth command high levels of support. If Alt's 'altruism thesis' is to be accepted as an explanation of the link between perceptions of welfare spending and a decline in support for the welfare state at large, it must be borne in mind that this perception is confined to particular aspects of welfare and cannot apply to other areas.

These considerations suggest that it is important to distinguish the welfare benefits for the minority of undeserving poor who may batten on the sober industrious citizenry from the bulk of social spending which is directed to the needs of the mass of the population. Such spending may in fact be of most benefit to the well-off. The welfare backlash argument asserts that in the first area, the majority see the minority as an unjustified burden on their backs; in the second area concern at welfare spending as a whole is explained by an incorrect belief, possibly founded on over-generalisation from minority services, that the large-spending services also redistribute to others. In the Medway survey, an attempt was made to assess attitudes to the various welfare services separately, as well as in aggregate.

Table 2 summarises answers to a range of questions about the desirability of state provision of a number of welfare services and the way in which provision should be organised. The range of services is wide, including benefits in cash or kind, means-tested and non-means-tested, highly restricted or universally available and currently provided on a mass scale or only existing in particular areas. The questions concerned the fact of state provision itself, the possibilities of restriction by income-level, contribution record, origin of need, availability of family support and level of cash benefit. This enables a large number of aspects of support to be explored. The range of questions asked in respect of each benefit was varied to mitigate interview fatigue and to focus on issues which piloting of the questionnaire indicated were salient in many people's minds.

Different people are likely to have different degrees of awareness of the services mentioned, and may well interpret the restrictions presented in different ways. For these reasons the statistics in the table should not be taken as exact measures of popular support for the various services, but rather as indications of the general climate of popular ideas in relation to relatively ill-defined areas of welfare policy.

The responses do not correspond in any clear-cut way to evidence of how people react to welfare provision. For example there are strong demands for restriction of child benefit and day-care yet there is no evidence of any take-up problem for such provision. Many other factors in addition to attitudes influence behaviour.

A rough guide to the relative standing of different aspects of welfare along the various dimensions of opinion is provided by the rank-orderings. These are calculated so that services are only ranked differently when level of support varies significantly. Reference to these rank-orderings indicates a substantial consistency across the different dimensions of opinion in public attitude to the various services. In order to explore this homogeneity in opinion further, the sample was split up into a number of different ways: by social class position, age, gender, presence of children under sixteen in the household, tenure and political party support. Rank-orderings were then computed for each subgroup, so that the ordering of women could be compared with that of men, and so on. Again the picture of a substantial homogeneity of opinion emerged with the same services falling at the top and bottom end of the rank-ordering.

The evidence reinforces the view that a general climate of opinion exists among the public that strongly supports services for the elderly, the sick and disabled, education and the NHS, and is antipathetic to benefits for the unemployed, low paid, lone parents and children, with the other services occupying an intermediate position. Opinion is discerning between different needs but relatively homogeneous across the population. This account of the structure of public opinion is commonly found in social policy studies, whether explained in terms of stigma (Pinker, 1971), a distinction between deserving and undeserving groups (Jones, Brown and Bradshaw, 1979), the expression of work and family ethics (George and Wilding, 1972), of party support (Lewis, 1980) or of perceptions of need (Whiteley, 1981).

The division between the various need groups can be explained partially, but not entirely, in terms of antipathy to welfare for needy minorities as opposed to support for the two-thirds of state spending that is directed to the mass of the population. While unemployment, low pay and lone parenthood may plausibly be represented as such a burden, it is difficult to see how child benefit which most families gain at some time in their life is to have the same status. Conversely, while health care, education and pensions are mass services, the sick and disabled are a minority group which receive strong support. Thus, ideological judgments about

29

TABLE 2
Rank-orderings of judgments about how welfare services should be provided (N = 240)

Percentage agreeing that the service should be:

Service	provided by the state	available to all members of the need group	not restricted by income	not restricted by contribution record	not restricted by how one came to be in need	not restricted by available family support	at a level approaching an average average wage
Favoured services:							
Old age pension	99 (1=)	62 (2=)	63 (2=)	54 (3=)	–	92 (1=)	79 (1=)
Sick and disabled	98 (1=)	73 (2=)	60 (2=)	82 (1=)	–	–	82 (1=)
Old persons' homes	98 (1=)	75 (2=)	78 (1)	–	–	73 (3=)	–
Home care for the elderly	96 (1=)	64 (5=)	69 (2=)	–	–	42 (6)	–
Education	–	94 (1)	–	–	–	–	–
Widow's benefit	97 (1=)	56 (7)	39 (6=)	79 (1=)	–	90 (1=)	80 (1=)
National health							

Unemployment benefit	93 (6=)	31 (11=)	34 (9=)	40 (5=)	28 (3)	61 (5)	56 (5=)
Low paid benefit	72 (8=)	36 (11=)	28 (9=)	34 (5=)	72 (1)	–	50 (5=)
Lone parent benefit	90 (6=)	47 (8=)	12 (12=)	–	38 (2)	68 (4=)	76 (1=)
Council housing	–	45 (8=)	40 (6=)	–	–	–	–
Child benefit	71 (8=)	34 (11=)	31 (9=)	48 (3=)	–	–	–
Day care for pre-school children	62 (10)	42 (8=)	42 (6=)	–	–	–	–
Average	88	54	46	51	46	71	61

Note The numbers in brackets are rank-orderings; percentages which are not significantly differentiated by correlated T-tests at the 0.05 level are treated as of equal rank.

the desert of different groups are also likely to play a part.

The ideological distinction between favoured and unfavoured services is strongly supported by other evidence, and appears relatively consistent over time. Rudolf Klein, in an analysis of public opinion poll data from the early 1950s to the mid-1970s, shows that over the period 'by and large, there is a high degree of satisfaction with the services provided' by the welfare state. However,

> the nineteenth century distinction between the deserving and the undeserving poor seems to be alive and kicking . . . in the minds of a majority of people. With remarkable consistency over the years there is a very large majority which favours raising pensions, and a very large minority which is highly critical of family allowance (Klein, 1974, pp. 410–11).

Education, the NHS and benefits for deserving groups receive strong support, in contrast to unemployment benefits and council housing. A study by Lipsey of polls for 1978 and 1979 reiterates the popularity of pensions and health services as against child and unemployment benefits (1979, p. 13). In a multivariate re-analysis of data from Butler and Stokes's October 1974 General Election Study, Whiteley concludes 'welfare spending is still popular among the great majority of the electorate': 'the general climate of public opinion in Britain will not accept a fundamental dismantling of the welfare state, as distinct from its erosion at the edges' (1981, p. 473). These findings are echoed in the work of Runciman (1972, p. 266), Abrams (1973, p. 27), Harris and Seldon (1979, p. 13), Norris (1978, p. 18), Schlackman (1978, p. 34), Golding and Middleton (1982, pp. 169–70), Lewis (1980, p. 289), Hockley and Harbour, (1982, p. 11) and in Coughlin's discussion of UK opinion polls from 1958 to 1969 (1980, pp. 66 and 69). These surveys cover a considerable time-span and use questions phrased in different ways, posed in the context of different surveys. It is hard to doubt that the distinction between favoured and unfavoured provision is a major ingredient in popular attitudes to welfare, and that it is held with remarkable homogeneity by the public.

This distinctive UK pattern is also apparent in the United States where Feagin's 1969 study shows a strong individualist and punitive attitude to the poor (1975, ch. 3). However, this is compatible with attitudes which suggest very strong support for universal state welfare systems according to a survey conducted with a sample of over nine thousand in seven states in 1972/3. The co-existence of strong negative stereotypes of some groups of the poor with equally strong support for welfare is explained by the argument that 'public opinion seems to withhold patronage only from those it regards as indifferent, wasteful or somehow abusive of values held by the majority' (Carter, Fifield and Shields, 1973, pp. 25 and 29; see also Curtin and Cowan, 1975).

A similar picture emerges in F. L. Cooke's study of support for various kinds of provision for a range of need groups in Chicago:

> public preferences appear, in general, to be more favourable towards supporting some groups than others. Overall, the disabled receive more support than the poor and support seems to be greater the more serious the poverty and disability. Also the elderly receive more support than do children and adults under 65 (1979, p. 155).

The deserving/undeserving distinction is widely supported. At the same time the public discriminate precisely and consistently between need groups *and* between needs for different services: 'the question the . . . public seems to be asking is "deserving of what?" rather than "are they deserving?"' (ibid., p. 174).

There is considerable evidence for the view, despite the moralistic tinge of scroungerphobia which is evident in many media reports (Golding and Middleton, 1982, pp. 59–108; Deacon, 1978, p. 120) and the prevalent negative stereotypes of some groups of poor (Townsend, 1979, pp. 427–8) that the public supports most state welfare and especially the large spending areas. One of the most striking features of the distinction between favoured and unfavoured groups is the homogeneity of opinion across the population: the studies by Klein, Golding, Lewis, Harris, Carter and Cooke show that the groups most likely to suffer the needs accounted undeserving express very little more support for welfare in these areas. This is highlighted in Golding's work, which contrasts an area with a history of high unemployment with a relatively prosperous city. Little difference is found in attitudes to the causes of poverty or the legitimacy of poor relief (p. 198).

The overall pattern of opinion is that of a public which is homogeneous and discriminating in its general attitudes to welfare services. The picture of mounting antagonism to welfare is only sustained if attention is concentrated on attitudes to particular unfavoured needs. These do not provide an adequate guide to opinions about the range of welfare services as a whole. In any case, the historical dimension provided by Klein's work provides little support for the view that anti-welfare sentiment is increasing markedly in the medium term, even in the areas of unfavoured provision.

The survey also considered the general pattern of support for the welfare state as a whole rather than as an aggregate of services for different groups. Attitudes in this area display an ambivalence which parallels that in support for particular services. There are two sources in the questionnaire for this conclusion: responses to general questions about welfare in the abstract and subjective judgments about the impact of welfare on the individual.

In the first area people were invited to agree or disagree with a series of statements about the effect that 'the system of taxes, services and benefits that many people call the welfare state' has on society as a whole. These questions were asked towards the end of the questionnaire when the individual had had the opportunity to discuss the range of services and various non-state alternatives in some detail. Table 3 gives the pattern of responses. The statements used were culled by content analysis from thirty-six discursive pre-pilot interviews. These interviews ranged over the whole area of people's judgments about state welfare. The opinions expressed employ prescriptive and emotive language, are in many cases phrased in a leading manner and imply judgments about the scope and weaknesses of state welfare. They are designed to allow individuals to locate themselves in relation to major currents in opinion, rather than to evaluate attitudes along a pre-selected, comprehensive and balanced set of dimensions. The sphere of overall judgments may be compared with that of specific opinions about particular services.

The pattern of opinions expressed in the attitude statements is necessarily complex. It may be conveniently summarised by considering support for propositions that suggest that the welfare state undermines particular values and positive opinions about state welfare. In the first area, majority support for the view that the welfare state encourages community support and altruism is lacking (statements A, C, E). There is also no support for the suggestion that it is egalitarian, efficient and unobtrusive (G, M, N, S, X). It tends to foster stigma and social division (K, U). This picture contradicts the ideal of social welfare associated with the fabian tradition in this country (see George and Wilding, 1976, ch. 4). The view that welfare undermines the work ethic, saps self-help and supports the undeserving is also favoured (B, F, O, Z). However, there is no strong support for the view that it attacks the values of the family ethic (H, Q). In addition, there is evidence of generalised attitudinal support for the welfare state as a desirable institution in principle (L, R, V, W, Y). Dissatisfaction at existing

TABLE 3
Value judgments on the welfare state (%: N = 240)

The system of taxes and benefits that many people call the welfare state:

		Agree	Neutral	Disagree
A	Makes people more ready to help each other	20	10	70
B	Makes people less willing to look after themselves	61	13	27
C	Makes for a more caring society	28	12	60
D	Costs too much in tax	43	14	44
E	Gives people the satisfaction of helping others they don't know	33	18	49
F	Saps the will to work	60	9	31
G	Makes people more equal	30	6	64
H	Makes people less ready to look after their relatives	50	13	37
I	Meets people's needs satisfactorily	28	15	58
J	Doesn't provide enough in benefits and services	54	16	30
K	Makes people who get benefit and services feel like second-class citizens	48	10	42
L	Is more or less fair	47	15	38
M	Has too many rules and regulations	70	10	20
N	Doesn't affect most people much	27	10	63
O	Helps people who don't deserve help	71	13	17
P	Gives most people value for money	48	12	41
Q	Makes people take less responsibility for their children	40	11	49
R	Is good in principle but needs reform	93	4	3
S	Helps the working class more than the middle class	36	15	49
T	Is something most people don't feel very involved in	69	11	20
U	Causes bad feeling between taxpayers and people who get benefits and services	68	8	25
V	Is necessary in a modern society	84	6	10
W	Gives people a greater sense of security	68	9	23
X	Interferes too much in people's lives	31	9	60
Y	Makes for a just society	38	21	41
Z	Helps people who don't need help	70	8	21

TABLE 4
Value for money from the welfare state

(a) Kinds of households thought to get the best value for money from the system of taxes and benefits taken as a whole (%)

	High income	Middle income	Low income	Other	Number
Whole sample	27	13	31	28	240
£5,500 or less	36	9	21	35	58
£5,501 – £8,499	30	17	24	29	103
£8,500 or more	16	11	47	25	79

(b) Taking all the benefits, services and taxes we have talked about together, do you think you get value for money from the welfare state? (%)

	Yes	No	Number
Whole sample	59	41	240
£5,500 or less	47	53	58
£5,501 – £8,499	69	31	103
£8,500 or more	54	46	79

achievements could lead to demands for the improvement instead of the dismantling of social policy. This interpretation is reinforced by the support for many aspects of welfare detailed earlier, and by the strong approval of the principle of state welfarism. It is also reinforced by the evidence on attitudes to private welfare discussed earlier. The findings do offer some support for the view that popular attitudes correspond to the disillusion with the current achievements of collective welfare evident among intellectuals. They do not suggest that 'welfare backlash' is a dominant opinion.

The second set of evidence about general attitudes derives from questions designed to explore opinions about the general effect of welfare. Respondents were asked 'which households would you say get the best value for money from the system of taxes and benefits taken as a whole?' The top row of Table 4 gives the responses. It can be seen that these stand in sharp contrast to the picture presented by Golding and Middleton of a 'widespread belief in the disincentive effect of over-generous or laxly-monitored welfare benefits' (1982, p. 176). However, questions of wider scope present a different perspective. The proportion of the sample who saw the welfare state as a whole of greatest benefit to the less well off, is roughly equal to the proportion seeing it as helping high income groups most. Perhaps the evidence that welfare redistributes to the better off is not entirely dissonant with the everyday experience of most people. Cross-tabulation of this attitude with the respondent's own income shows a tendency to see the benefits as flowing to other groups than one's own. The poor think the better off get the gravy and vice versa. This indicates that, despite the support for the major services, a generalised sense of the whole system as a burden may be present.

The issue of value for money was then focussed on individual experience. Respondents were also asked if they felt that they themselves got value for money from 'the system of taxes and social services taken as a whole'. This perception is most strongly evident among the middle income respondents and less prominent among both low and high income groups, indicating that dissatisfaction with welfare is strongest at the extremes of the income distribution.

Cross-tabulation of attitude variables with measures of class, age and other personal circumstances revealed a pattern comparable to that of the judgments about particular services. There were few strong relationships. The overall impression is of a homogeneous structure of attitudes throughout the population. The pattern formed by the relationship of opinions on different state services within this consistent structure is of interest, particularly as it bears on the argument that there has been a shift in public support away from the welfare state.

The keynote of the analysis of general attitudes is of ambivalence in support for the welfare state. There is strong support for the principle of state welfare but concern at its practice. There is a widespread feeling of disquiet at welfare as a public burden. The pattern of attitudes at large is relatively homogeneous across the population as is the case with perceptions of particular services. The strongest link with the overall judgments of support for welfare is with personal satisfaction at the 'value for money' gained from the system.

The evidence does not support the suggestion that the mass of the population has recently turned against the welfare state. This is likely to be based on over-generalisation from perceptions of minority services. The historical data presented by Klein reinforces the view that the most salient feature of attitudes in this area is of continuity over time. The high-spending services for the mass of the population are supported by most people. Despite this there is some evidence of a general concern at the operation of the welfare state in relation to cherished values and at its redistributive aspects. How does this relate to the second claim of new crisis theory, that there is popular support for the denationalisation of state welfare services?

Support for private market provision

The expansion of the private sector in welfare is a major policy aim of the 1979 and 1983 Conservative governments. 'The balance of our society has been increasingly titled in favour of the state: this election may be the last chance we have to reverse that process', Mrs Thatcher wrote in her introductory statement to the 1979 manifesto (1979, p. 1). Does this reflect the pattern in popular demands?

The strongest evidence of popular preferences for market welfare comes from a series of studies commissioned by the Institute of Economic Affairs. Since the findings have occasioned considerable controversy and important issues of method are raised, the most recent will be discussed in some detail. The central argument is that:

> it is no longer possible to doubt that the representative samples of varying ages, sex, social and occupational and educational background, and apparently contrasting political sympathy reflect a growing preference – showed by a clear majority in 1978 – for changes in policy that would enable families to choose education and health services outside the state (Harris and Seldon, 1979, p. 201).

The welfare state is seen as an agency of coercion, forcing people to pay taxes to finance collective services which they would prefer to buy as individuals in a market system. This thesis, it is claimed, is supported by evidence in three main areas.

First, four-fifths of the sample opposed the policy of preventing people from 'paying extra for themselves for services they need' outside the welfare state. The proportion is not markedly different for the various age, sex, and class groups, and political party supporters. Secondly, there is considerable support for state voucher systems to enable people to buy private health care and education. About half the sample would be prepared to make up the value of a 50 per cent health care voucher. Other evidence also suggests unsatisfied demand for private welfare provision. A feasibility study on education vouchers in Ashford found that over two-thirds of parents felt denied adequate choice of school in the state system and would welcome the opportunity to use vouchers (Kent County Council, 1978, ch. 4). Thirdly, people were asked whether they would be prepared to pay more tax to finance increases in welfare spending. Fewer than half the sample were willing to do so.

Thus the study provides evidence of strong support for private welfare and of the limits to support for the welfare state. This impression is reinforced by the democratic success at the 1979 and 1983 elections of a party identified with control of welfare expenditure, and by the lack of sustained mass opposition to welfare cuts. Moreover, recent years have seen considerable expansions in private health insurance where membership of schemes has roughly doubled between 1971 and 1983 and occupational pensions where the numbers covered have increased from 50 to over 60 per cent of the labour force over the same period (Central Statistical Office, 1984, p. 111; Ritchie, 1983, p. 13). This evidence must be treated with caution for three reasons. Firstly, the expansion of these schemes is in large measure the outcome of negotiations between corporate bodies such as trade unions and employers, and the balance of advantage may be influenced by government fiscal and wages policies and the desire to control aspects of the lives of the workforce. Secondly, both areas receive very considerable subsidies from the state (see Field, 1981, pp. 159–85). In this sense, current expansion may be better seen as a change in the form of state welfare, rather than a shift away from collective provision. Thirdly, the expansion does not seem to be paralleled in the case of education, despite considerable public subsidies. This suggests that forces other than straightforward support for private provision may be involved. However, it seems unlikely that the expansion of private welfare through occupational enrolment would take place without the passive compliance at the least of the workforce, which indicates that private welfare is not actively opposed.

In the Medway study, the questionnaire explored respondents' knowledge of private welfare, their perceptions of its effect on society and on recipients and their preferences between private and public provision. The principal focus was on education and health care services, although some questions were asked about occupational and private insurance pensions and home ownership, and state subsidies for them through the fiscal system.

There was a high degree of awareness of the existence of private schemes: all of the sample had heard of private education; 84 per cent of 'private health insurance schemes', like BUPA, for example; and 93 per cent of occupational pension schemes.

Membership of such schemes varied: 12 per cent were members of private health insurance schemes; 7 per cent had been to independent schools themselves and 7 per cent had children at such schools; and 49 per cent were members of occupational pension schemes. Men and members of higher income groups were much more likely to be members of private schemes.

To explore the issues of popular support for private welfare two kinds of questions were used, to distinguish opinions about the principle of private provision from personal preferences between state and market. The first concerns popular tolerance for contracting out of the welfare state. To escape the problem of accounting for the effect of preference for private market provision by some groups on the position of those continuing to use state services, the viability of the principle of contracting out was assumed. In addition, motives for choice and their relation to need were ignored. The questions asked: 'should people be allowed to stop paying towards (the relevant state service) and choose (the relevant private service) if they want to?' The pattern of responses is largely similar to that found by Harris and Seldon. About three-quarters of the sample approve the principle of tolerance of the right to contract out of state welfare for private education and health-care provision and occupational pension schemes. The slightly lower level of support may be due to the different wording of the question. The most striking feature of the responses is their homogeneity. There is little relation to class or income which might be connected to capacity to pay for private provision. The only significant associations (at the 0.05 level by chi-squared) revealed by cross-tabulation with social and political variables are rather greater support by women for tolerance in all three areas, by Conservative supporters in relation to education and pensions and by those with dependent children for education. The relation with gender is not immediately obvious. It is interesting that party identification does not relate to tolerance in the field of private health care.

The second strand to exploration of market preference attempted to elicit more concrete choices. In the case of health care and education respondents were asked 'if it cost you the same to use state as private provision which would you choose?' The questions were designed to evade the difficulties of evaluating the relative direct and indirect costs of different voucher and other schemes. They were asked at the end of the sections on private provision so that respondents would already have considered aspects of private and state provision. In addition, people were asked if all firms should run occupational pension schemes.

In the case of health care and education, majorities of about two-thirds chose private provision. Low income and manual groups and Labour supporters expressed weaker preferences (significant at the 0.05 level by chi-squared), but in no category did less than 55 per cent favour the market option. Interest and political affiliation play a minor role in determining attitudes. The impression of a homogeneous opinion favouring market welfare is reinforced.

A follow-up question asking reasons for choice in the case of health care found those who chose the NHS split roughly two-thirds/one-third between the ground of previous favourable experience of treatment (63 per cent) and the argument that state health services need support (36 per cent); those who chose private provision did so mainly on the grounds that standards were better (51 per cent) or that service was quicker (38 per cent). Dissatisfaction with the NHS played a small role (9 per cent) and appeals to an ideal of free choice in the market were relatively insignificant (2 per cent). It seems likely that it is a calculus of self-interest based on life-experience and belief rather than values about the role of state and market that is important in this area. The question about occupational pension provision indicated strong overall support (89 per cent) very slightly more evident among manuals, lower income households and Conservatives.

Further questions on the desirability of fiscal support for private services were asked later in the questionnaire. These showed strong support for tax relief on private pension and insurance schemes (60 per cent of the sample) and even stronger support for tax relief on mortgage interest payments (85 per cent) largely indifferentiated by social group or political support. A follow-up showed that most respondents favoured mortgage interest relief as a subsidy because they got it or were likely to (64 per cent). Only 6 per cent argued that this helped needy groups such as first-time buyers and 26 per cent argued in more abstract terms that owner-occupation reduced the burden on direct state provision of council housing. Seventy per cent of the minority who opposed mortgage relief thought that the subsidy was unfair to those who could not afford to buy. As in the case of private health care, opinions about subsidies seem to relate closely to ideas about self-interest. This appears to provide some support for Dunleavy's view that self-interest links with consumption sector location and thus with demands for state subsidy.

An interesting issue concerns the relation between support for public and private welfare. Many writers see state and market in opposition in the way that some politicians suggest that 'rolling back the frontiers of the state' and 'expansion of the market' are synonymous. Thus Harris and Seldon's concern at the expansion of the state is rooted in the belief that there is popular support for more private services, and this implies less welfare state. How is the evidence of support for the mass welfare state services *and* for the private sector presented so far to be reconciled?

Harris and Seldon argue that the failure in many surveys of satisfaction with state welfare to provide clear statements of the price to respondents of the choices they are being asked to make leads to confusion. From their standpoint this precisely reflects the political practice of the welfare state in which politicians often have an interest in concealing from citizens the cost of attractive manifestos to secure support. Alternatives must be priced to reflect the realities of public choice.

While surveys such as those of Butler and Stokes in 1963 and 1966 pose tax reduction and spending on services as simple alternatives (1971, pp. 468 and 498) more recent studies such as the 1976 Eurobarometer survey and Gallup polls since 1975 point out to the respondent that cutting tax means cutting services and vice versa (Coughlin, 1980, p. 134; R. Rose, 1983, p. 15). Perhaps the most sophisticated approach is contained in a postal survey carried out in 1980, which asked respondents to allocate 'fiscal vouchers' between tax cuts and service spending (Hockley and Harbour, 1982). The results from all these studies are not markedly dissimilar. Critics of the 1960s approach argue that the pricing of voucher alternatives to state provision in the IEA study is unsatisfactory since the issues of the finance of the voucher, respondent's preferences for welfare provision for those who are unable to enter the welfare market and the extent of provision funded by the voucher are not discussed (Golding and Middleton, 1982, p. 156; Forsyth, 1966, p. 93). However, it seems that data from other studies supports the general contention of a demand for private welfare suppressed by governmental coercion. Conversely, evidence of satisfaction with state services reported by Klein and others seems immune to this criticism. People's reports of satisfaction may become more muted when the burden of taxation is introduced, yet there still appear to be majorities in favour of most state provision.

In order to make clear to respondents to the Medway study the fact that provision means taxation a series of questions were asked in relation to eight services to find out whether people supported changes in expenditure and were ready to pay for what they wanted. A baseline of current expenditure was provided on a card given to the respondent, expressed as the number of pounds out of

TABLE 5
Support for changes in expenditure on welfare services (%; N = 240)

Service	Current expenditure per £100	The level of expenditure should be			Support for more expenditure even if it means more tax
		less	the same	more	
Sick and disabled benefits	£5	2	42	56	50
National health service	£20	11	36	53	48
State education	£20	8	48	44	40
Single parent benefits	£2	5	52	43	35
Old age pension	£25	6	63	31	26
Council housing	£10	17	54	29	20
Unemployment benefit	£5	10	62	28	18
Child benefit	£7	34	54	12	8

Note: The figures in the 'Current Expenditure' column were calculated from *The Government's Expenditure Plans, 1980–1 to 1983–4*, Cmnd 7841, HMSO, 1980, Tables 2:7, 2:10, 2:11 and 2:12.

each £100 spent on welfare going to each service. This communicated a rough idea of the relative cost of current provision and thus the relative fiscal impact of changes in that provision. The answers (Table 5) give a more concrete measure of support than that provided in Table 2.

Very few respondents favoured reductions in expenditure, except in the case of child benefit where the proportion was one-third. The rank-ordering of support loosely reflected that of support for provision and was more closely related to order of restrictions (Spearman's coefficient .77, significant at the .01 level). It correlated highly with the ranking of corresponding services in the IEA study in order of support for more expenditure (coefficient .90, significance level .01) (Harris and Seldon, 1979, p. 129). Considerable proportions of those who favoured more expenditure were willing to pay more in tax – the lowest proportions being for unfavoured services, such as child and unemployment benefit. Even here over half of those who supported more expenditure reported willingness to find the money.

This evidence indicates considerable support for the welfare state, both the principle of provision and the concrete level of willingness to pay tax. The rank-order correlations indicate that preferences for expenditure and restriction correlate more highly with each other than either does with abstract support for the provision of the service. Moral notions of desert on the one hand and practical considerations of financial self-interest on the other may combine to moderate support for welfare. The directions of such influence seem parallel, perhaps because the moral outgroups also constitute relative minorities.

The relation between these opinions and variables that related to need and political identification were then explored. The work of Whiteley indicated that these two factors are the best predictors of scores on a welfare spending index produced by re-analysis of the 1974 General Election Survey data (1981, p. 467). First, the data was dichotomised between social and political subgroups and rank-order correlation coefficients were computed to compare the orderings among high income and low income and manual and non-manual households; men and women; those over and under forty; those with and without dependent children; and conservative and Labour party supporters, along the dimensions of support for the existence of benefits; for restriction to some members of the relevant need group; and for more public expenditure on them. In all cases the coefficients between orderings by each value of the social variables were in excess of .85 and significant at the 0.05 level. This confirms the impression of homogeneity of opinion about the relative priority of different needs among groups that might plausibly be expected to have differing interests, or to be influenced by different political ideologies.

A more detailed examination involving cross-tabulation indicated a number of significant relations (by chi-squared at the 0.05 level). These seem to be plausibly related to ideas of interest in the particular service. For example, age and the presence of dependent children in the household relate most strongly to enthusiasm for unrestricted child benefit, and more expenditure on education; income and class relate to restrictions and expenditure; women support the provision of child benefit and expenditure on single parents' benefit; manual workers support council housing; and political party supporters follow party principles, especially in relation to services for traditionally undeserving groups. Opinions follow a complex pattern which is clearly influenced by personal circumstances. The pattern, however, is a subtheme: the dominant note is the overall consistency of ordering between the various subgroups. Opinions about state welfare display the strong homogeneous public support that Klein and Whiteley identify in this country and Cooke and Fifield in the United States of America, especially for high-spending services for deserving needs. The study went on to analyse the relation between support for public and private welfare by cross-tabulating attitudes to public and to private provision. Those who wish to use evidence of support for the private sector as ammunition for an attack on the welfare state (like Harris and Seldon) or as an indication that substantial changes are called for (like Bosanquet) assume that attitudes to market and state are in a contradictory relation. Thus opposition to the state is taken to imply support for the market and vice versa. The pattern of the data indicates that attitudes are more complex.

Opinions were examined in three areas – health care, education and pensions – corresponding to most peoples' experience of alternatives to the welfare state. Opinions about state welfare were dichotomised between support for increases and other attitudes in order to give a relatively strong measure of attitudes to expenditure. The relatively large numbers in the sample who wanted the level of expenditure maintained could be plausibly explained by inertia on the part of the respondent or an unwillingness to commit oneself to a particular opinion. Support for private provision was measured along two dimensions for health care and education: tolerance of contracting out at the level of principle, and concrete preferences for private services for oneself. Only the former question was asked about occupational pensions. Forty-nine per cent of the sample were in such schemes, but piloting indicated that concrete preferences were difficult to elicit, because most people saw membership as a matter of collective negotiation rather than individual choice. Table 6 shows the results. The striking point is that in only one out of the five tables displayed is there a significant relation between support for state and non-state provision. This is in the case of concrete preferences for private health care. Since the NHS which provides care free at the point of demand (in many cases) is often regarded as 'the most socialist of the social services' this is the area in which the most prominent differences should be expected. Yet even here 42 per cent of the sample either supported state expenditure yet would choose private care or vice versa.

TABLE 6
Support for public and private health care, education and pension
provision – the Medway findings (%)

			Spending on state provision should be increased:		
1 Education			*Yes*	*No*	*Overall*
The level of principle	Tolerant of contracting out	Yes	74	73	73
		No	26	27	27
			Chi-squared=0.47; probability=0.81		
Concrete Preference	Would prefer private service	Yes	63	65	64
		No	37	35	36
	Number*		97	139	236
			Chi-squared= .54; probability=0.75		
2 Health care					
The level of principle	Tolerant of contracting out	Yes	67	75	71
		No	33	25	29
			Chi-squared=1.67; probability= .15		
Concrete preference	Would prefer private service	Yes	48	66	58
		No	52	34	42
	Number*		96	104	200
			Chi-squared=6.93; probability= .01		
3 Pensions					
The level of principle	Tolerant of contracting out	Yes	67	70	69
		No	33	30	31
	Number*		70	149	219
			Chi-squared=0.73; probability=0.38		

*Screening questions were asked to check respondent's awareness of the existence of private provision.

The complexity of the relation between support for public and private care is borne out in re-analysis of the IEA's own data set. While this does not contain direct questions about support for state welfare which may be contrasted with support for the private sector, data is available on attitudes to the public sector. One concern of the study was with the unresponsiveness of supposedly representative government to what people really want. This argument derives from the claim by writers like Niskanen (1971) that the advanced capitalist state is more responsive to well-organised producer interests, not least in its own bureaucracies, than to relatively diffuse consumer demands. In addition, recent analysis of the workings of democracy by public choice theorists demonstrates that it is entirely possible for the outcome of a ballot to be support for policies that few people actually want because opposition to the most cherished policies of particular groups may cancel itself out (Riker, 1982, ch. 2).

The IEA study accordingly asked people questions about how they would like expenditure on seven main areas of government activity redistributed. The areas were: retirement pensions, the NHS, council housing, education, unemployment benefit, defence and road building. Not surprisingly the preferences of ordinary citizens turn out to be 'clearly different from the political priorities imposed by the decisions of governments' (Harris and Seldon, 1979, p. 130). The extent of the coercion implicit in the use of taxpayers' money need not concern us here. The interesting point is that a measure of support for spending on state welfare, as opposed to non-welfare items, may be derived from the evidence. A two-value variable was constructed to measure support for state health care, distinguishing those who wanted more spent on this area of policy at the expense of non-welfare areas. Table 7 shows the relation between attitudes to state and market provision for health care in the IEA data – as we argued above the area where the two come into most striking opposition. The analysis contrasts support for redistribution from other areas of state activity to the NHS with support for health care vouchers and the principle of contracting out. As in the Medway survey data, there is no significant relation. Opinions about private and public provisions are not located at opposite ends of a single dimension, nor do they stand in a contradictory relation which obeys a simple law of excluded middle. Harris and Seldon move from their evidence of a 'growing preference . . . for changes in policy that would enable families to choose education and health services outside the state' to the claim that 'state spending . . . on schools and health services . . . increasingly fails to reflect the wishes' of the electorate (1979, pp. 201–2). This is to overrun their evidence. The similar pattern of findings from the 1981 Medway study indicates that state and private sector do not stand in simple opposition in public opinion, and that the use of the IEA's data as evidence of declining support for the welfare state is therefore misleading. Similarly, the transition made by Whiteley from evidence 'that welfare spending is still popular among the great majority of the electorate' to the view that 'the general climate of public opinion . . . will not accept a fundamental dismantling of the

TABLE 7
Support for public and private health care – the IEA findings (%)

1

The level of principle

People who want to should not be allowed to pay extra for themselves for services they need outside the NHS

		Agree	Neutral	Disagree	Don't know	Overall
Support re-allocation to the NHS from other areas of state spending	Yes	74	68	65	61	67
	No	25	32	35	39	33
	Number	254	104	1593	41	1992

Chi-squared = 7.67; probability = 0.85

2

Concrete preferences

Would accept a voucher covering 50% of assumed private health insurance costs

		Yes	No	Don't know	Overall
Support re-allocation to the NHS from other areas of state spending	Yes	66	67	69	66
	No	34	33	31	34
	Number	1012	841	139	1992

Chi-squared = 0.51; probability = 0.78

welfare state' (1981, p. 473) may also be illusory. The analysis of the ambiguities and contradictions in public opinion indicates that we can talk neither of a simple shift to the right against the welfare state, nor of whole-hearted support for it.

We move on to consider the third theme in new crisis theory's discussion of attitudes – the question of how far the current of opinion contradicts the gains made by women.

Welfare and women

It is noticeable that in the general homogeneity of support for state welfare there are no marked associations with sex, apart from women's support for more state spending. Women also show greater tolerance for opting out to private health care and education, but less support for fiscal subsidies for mortgages and private pension schemes. This may be explicable by a simple notion of individual self-interest, since the women in the sample were less likely to be taxpayers or to have mortgages than the men. However they are equally likely to be members of households affected by these systems. The issue of the effect of current policies on women's interests was explored in more depth in relation to specific topics.

Feminist discussion of the impact of changes in the welfare state on women has centred mainly on the assumptions made about the dependency of women in the family and their consequent availability to care for dependent groups (for example, Land, 1978, p. 257; Ungerson, 1982, p. 1; Rose and Rose, 1982, p. 8; Finch and Groves, 1980, p. 487). Changes in demographic and employment patterns over the last twenty years are imposing fresh pressures on women. The collision is between the expansion in the numbers of single parents coupled with the demand for community care for the elderly and other dependent groups and the increased tendency for women – especially married women – to enter paid employment. Consequently the questions asked in the Medway study concerned two areas: state care for dependants and social security for lone parents. These issues have not been explored in depth in other surveys, although there is some work on attitudes to community care (Cooke, 1979; West, Illsley and Kelman, 1984).

The section of the questionnaire which explored attitudes to dependants on the family was described 'as about services the government might provide so that women would have less to do in looking after dependent members of the family'. Attention was concentrated deliberately and overtly on the role of women as carers. Three particular issues were picked out. There was considerable support for day care for pre-school children, for home care services for the elderly and for residential accommodation for them. In each case there was majority support for universal availability ('to all who want them') and opposition to means-testing (Table 2).

Day care was valued as much for its social and educational benefits as for its capacity to release women for work. There was support for restricting home care services for the elderly only to those not living with their families, but little enthusiasm for restricting residential care in this way. This furnishes evidence of substantial minority allegiance to a family ethic despite the level of support for state provision of services. This is borne out by detailed examination for replies to an open-ended question probing reasons for support for the service. Forty-seven per cent of those who wanted state child care favoured it on the grounds that it aided the development of the child, rather than that it helped women who worked. Nearly 30 per cent of those who wanted home support for the elderly favoured it for the reason that this group was better off with their family. This coincides with the overall judgments given in response to general questions about

49

the impact of the welfare state on family life (Table 3): half the sample thought the welfare state 'makes people less ready to look after their relatives' (against 37 per cent who disagreed – statement H). Forty per cent thought 'it makes people take less responsibility for their children' against 49 per cent who took the opposite view (statement Q).

These statements and the specific opinions about particular services were all cross-tabulated with sex and presence of dependent children, but did not show any significant relationship except in the case of the follow-up questions about old person's home provision. Those with dependent children were significantly more likely to favour the provision of this service without restriction by means-test or the availability of relatives to care for the elderly person. Attitudes to the family and welfare appear as a general ideology without any clear recognition of interest associated with sex. The level of support for day care for pre-school children indicates that enthusiasm for this service (which has never existed on a large scale in the welfare state, and which constituted one of the first four demands of the women's movement) is widespread.

This finding parallels that of an extensive study of attitudes to community care in Scotland. This survey developed the issue of support for care in the community and concluded: 'what the public want is not care *by* the community, nor residential care except in specific circumstances, but a range of community-based services which best serve the interests of dependency groups and alleviate the burden on carers . . . it is advocacy of a continued partnership between the family and the welfare state, in which the former does not replace the latter' (West, Illsley and Kelman, 1984, p. 17).

Opinions about two welfare benefits of special relevance to women (a single parent's benefit and widow's benefit) were explored. Ninety per cent of single parents are single and no specific benefit exists for this group, although the Finer Committee recommended a means-tested Guaranteed Maintenance Allowance in 1974 and demands for this measure have re-echoed ever since.

Both widow's and single parent's benefits received strong support (from 98 per cent and 90 per cent of the sample respectively: Table 2). The difference lies in attitudes to the organisation of benefits. Just over half of those who thought there should be a lone parent benefit wanted it restricted on specific criteria, as against 44 per cent for widow's benefit. The difference became more striking as particular systems of restriction were explored. Nearly 90 per cent wanted lone parent's benefit restricted by income level as against 60 per cent for widow's benefit. The availability of family support was seen as more important in deciding levels of lone parent than widow's benefit, although in both cases considerable majorities thought this irrelevant.

A similar question on support was asked in relation to retirement pension and unemployment benefit, with majority opposition to restriction of benefit if family support were available in all cases. Support for the encroachment of state welfare on the family ethic, as far as social security goes, seems considerable. A further aspect of social security dependency was explored in relation to unemployment benefit. This is the system whereby couples are considered as a unit for the purposes of the system and benefit paid to the husband for both (unless the wife has a separate contribution record, in which case she will receive benefit for herself while he gets his own benefit and dependant's allowance for children). The question asked 'in cases where both are unemployed, should the benefit be paid to the husband or to the wife?' A small majority (53 per cent of those who answered) favoured the wife as recipient, contradicting official practice.

Overall, it seems that the thesis that a powerful family ethic demands that women remain in the home available to care for children and other dependants and that their social security rights should be related to their position in the family, is not supported. However there is a moderate measure of enthusiasm for restricting state services so that the primary responsibilities of families for elderly relatives and young children are not eroded, and some general concern at the extent to which the welfare state under-mines family commitment to care. The questions asked here only scrape the surface of the area, which has been little explored. The fact that opinions do not relate closely to gender indicates that an overall ideology rather than a particular interest is being ex-pressed. The pattern of homogeneity found in other areas of opinions is again evident.

Conclusion

This review of evidence on people's attitudes to public welfare, privatisation and welfare for women indicates that there has been no strong shift against the welfare state. To the contrary the main services are as strongly supported as they have been at any time since the war.

The accounts of welfare backlash appear to be based on

extrapolation from particular areas of the welfare state in which there is popular concern, or from the incorrect assumption that support for the market implies antagonism to the state. This disquiet is not the main theme occurring through the pattern of attitudes as a whole.

The structure of opinion is complex. The dominant note is one of ambivalence along two dimensions. Support for the mass welfare state services of pensions, the NHS and education is tempered by concern at unemployment and low-pay benefits, council housing and lone parent's benefits. Perceptions of redistribution and of the welfare state as a whole show strong support for the principle of state welfare with some concern at the cost and the extent of transfer to other groups. This is the only justification for the 'welfare burden' model in public opinion.

The second dimension concerns the balance of support for both public and private sectors. The welfare state seems to attract homogeneous support among all social groups, even those party supporters and class and tenure groups who also have a tendency to favour the private sector.

In the area of welfare for women there is some ambivalence between a generalised concern at the impact of the state system and the family ethic. This does not feed through into opinions about collective care for the elderly or pre-school children, or rules for the administration of benefits. Thus the ideological attack on the welfare state in the 1970s does not appear successful at the level of opinion. The strand of popular support for public provision is by no means threadbare. Moreover, such evidence as we have suggests that moralistic concern about some aspects of state spending is not a new phenomenon, but one which has existed throughout the history of the welfare state.

3

From Butskellism to the new right?

'Hegel wrote somewhere that history repeats itself . . . he
forgot to add the first time as tragedy, the second time as farce'
Karl Marx, *The Eighteenth
Brumaire of Louis Napoleon*

This chapter seeks to relate the pattern of public opinion about
welfare issues discussed in chapters 1 and 2 to the development of
the welfare state. The Medway survey evidence demonstrated a
strong division in popular attitudes between support for the
favoured high-spending state services and the unfavoured services
catering for minorities. The pattern of support is consistent both in
judgments about the scope of provision and in willingness to pay
for services. Comparison with data from British Election Studies,
with Klein's review of opinion polls since the war and with other
sources indicates that the structure of opinions is broadly
consistent over time. It seems likely that excessive concentration
on the unfavoured services had led some writers to the view that
there is a radical change in opinion. The perception of self-interest
in provision seems an important determinant of opinion although
the pattern of attitudes is complex.

In this sense, the view that there is a division in support for state
and welfare is reinforced. The other issues identified as central to
new right rhetoric on welfare in chapter 1 – the paradoxical
dependence of women as unpaid care-workers in families, and the
celebration of private market welfare – do not appear to strike a
resonant response in popular attitudes. There is little evidence of a

consistent family ethic either in general value-judgments or in opinions about the organisation of particular services. Private and occupational welfare is strongly supported, but the pattern of opinion does not contradict support for the welfare state. It does not furnish an adequate basis for the claim that there is a popular demand to roll back the frontiers of state provision. Ideological judgments seem to be the most important factors underlying opinions in this area. The pattern of opinions about private welfare is difficult to test over time, since little attention has been paid to this issue. However, the consistency between the Medway study and the re-analysis of the IEA study in 1978 indicates some stability in opinions, at least in the recent past.

This work undermines the view that the current of public opinion has turned against the welfare state in the 1970s. The claim that the public currently reject the welfare state goes hand-in-hand with a version of the history of its development that harks back to a heritage of popular enthusiasm. This version has two aspects. First the story is told of a passage from political consensus to political conflict, from a bipartisan approval of welfare in the immediate post-war period, to an increasingly bitter party conflict over welfare issues arising in the mid-1960s and becoming ever more embracing as the 1970s progressed. This links to the second strand, which stresses the development of a mass ideology of the new right, manipulated and nurtured by populist politicians and gaining an increasing ascendency in the Conservative party from which it was able to carry out a systematic attack on the welfare state from 1979 onwards. This story is infected with nostalgia for the golden age of welfare consensus.

The claim advanced in this chapter is that the manifold changes of the welfare state over the post-war period do not amount to much in the way of difference. Firstly we discuss the post-war settlement and the period up to the mid-1960s, to show that many writers exaggerate the degree of political consensus in this period. The palmy days of the welfare state required effort in their production and struggle in their maintenance. Secondly, the importance of developing political controversy after 1964 may be less marked in its influence on the outcome of policy than is often suggested. Thirdly, throughout the post-war period, the welfare state has contained the main features of the new right politics enshrined as central principles of its organisation and practice.

The foundation of consensus: the post-war settlement

There are two important props which support the claim that the
post-war settlement and the continuance of Labour policies into
the 1951–64 Conservative government represented a triumph of
political consensus. Firstly, many of the social policies in the
closing years of the second war or immediately after it were the
fruit of bipartisan planning under war-time coalition or at any rate
were effectively unopposed by Conservative MPs. It is pointed out
that the Conservative party remade its social policy over the
period from 1942 with a grudging acceptance of the Beveridge
report in the 1943 debate, the embracing of Keynesian principles
of economic planning in the 'Industrial Charter' adopted at the
1947 party conference, and the endorsement of official reports
approving the bulk of the NHS, National Insurance and Social
Security reforms in the early 1950s. Secondly, in many areas the
Conservative government of the 1950s continued the patterns of
post-war Labour spending on the major social programmes. Let us
examine these claims in more detail.

The major legislative changes of the post-war settlement were
the 1945 Family Allowances Act, the 1946 National Insurance Act
and the 1948 National Assistance Act that gave force to the
Beveridge proposals in modified form; the 1944 Education Act
that established universal secondary education in an officially
tripartite but in practice bipartite form and the 1946 NHS Act.
War-time rent controls were retained, legislation regulating
planning passed in 1948 and a massive council house building
programme undertaken. These tackled the major housing short-
ages resulting from the bombardment of cities and the decay of six
years in which virtually no new houses had been completed.
Economic management techniques were developed with the
intention of maintaining high employment, although war-time
controls over raw materials and over retail consumption were
relaxed during the life of the government. The war-time structure
of mass PAYE taxation was retained so that the fiscal foundation
of total war became that of the welfare state.

The bulk of these policies were the fruit of bipartisan planning.
Beveridge's report is commonly seen more as the co-ordination of
existing demands by a wide range of groups than as the original
and radical document its Messianic style proclaims (Thane, 1982;
MacGregor, 1981, p. 8; Calder, 1969, p. 526). Nonetheless, it was
condemned by Churchill in a note to the cabinet as 'false hopes
and visions of Eldorado' (Jones et al., 1979, p. 48). It is probable

that the arthritic support of leading Conservatives in the 1943 debate on the report – in which they dwelt mainly on the implications of the proposals for higher taxes and insurance contributions – was an important factor in the 1945 Labour victory.

The 1944 Education Act built on pre-war trends. About 1 in 10 of all children went to private secondary schools in 1938. Of the remainder, 85 per cent attended elementary schools to the minimum leaving age of 14, 7 per cent went to selective state central schools with a technical bias and the same proportion to grammar schools. About half the recipients of state secondary education received scholarships to pay the fees. Most of those who passed the scholarship examinations were from middle-class backgrounds.

The 1938 Spens and 1943 Norwood reports recommended a tripartite division of secondary education into academic, technical and modern schooling. The Norwood report in particular is celebrated for its claim that children fell into these three natural ability-types, a claim much criticised by contemporary writers, including Sir Cyril Burt, the foremost contemporary authority on intelligence testing. The support of the Labour movement for the extension of secondary education to all children in tripartite form was lukewarm. However the realisation of the dream of secondary education for all (part of the Labour party platform since 1924) overcame reluctance to support divided education. The 1944 Act which raised the school leaving age to fifteen, extended secondary education to all and abolished fees in state schools received all-party support.

The National Health Service Act of 1946 enacted Beveridge's assumption of a universal, free NHS. It contained a compromise between Bevan's proposal of a unified service with salaried medical professionals and the interests of the hospitals and doctors' groups. Three nationally directed and financed systems were established, covering hospital services, GP services and local authority maternity, child care, health visiting and ambulance services. The influential teaching hospitals retained their endowments and a measure of autonomy. The majority of consultants who opted for part-time NHS appointments were free to pursue private practice. General Practitioners, part salaried, part paid through capitation fees, were also free to take private patients. The Act was opposed by Conservatives at the second reading on the grounds that it 'sought to impose upon the medical profession a form of discipline which . . . is totally unsuited to the practice of medicine, (Hansard, 30/4/46). Subsequent pressure from doctors' interests, reinforced by middle-class concern at the nationalisation of medicine and Conservative lobbying, forced an amending Act relinquishing direct salaries to GPs, and the abandonment of the principle that GP services should be provided through local authority-owned health centres.

Both parties promised crash housing programmes, continued private sector rent control and control of planning. Housing was a major issue in the 1945 election: Gallup polls indicated that four out of ten of the electorate identified housing as the most important single issue. Local authorities had built nearly a million houses by 1951, with the private sector contributing less than a quarter of that figure. Later policies indicate that a Conservative administration would have sought a different balance, although this is hard to demonstrate due to the absence of legislative debates and the reluctance of politicians to admit any criticism of policies that were providing housing in a period of acute shortage.

The principles of Keynesian economic management were largely accepted by the Treasury in the 1944 White Paper on Employment Policy, which called for 'sufficient state intervention in the economy to ensure a high and stable level of employment' and argued for the retention of war-time controls in the transition to peace. The approach was embodied in the 1947 Conservative 'Industrial Charter'. However, Conservative politicians repeatedly attacked the retention of rationing of consumer goods in the run up to the 1950 and 1951 elections and opposed the maintenance of war-time levels of direct taxation.

The implication of this discussion of major policy areas is that the 'Butskellite' consensus referred to by the *Economist* in 1953 was not achieved without effort. Moreover the appearance of bipartisan agreement on major social policy areas can only be produced by papering over real rifts in policy. Analysis of the record of the 1951–64 Conservative government leads to the same impression.

Three major reports on the working of the welfare state were received in the early 1950s: Phillips on Pensions (Cmd 9333, 1954); Guilleband on the NHS (Cmd 9663, 1956); and the Government Actuary's first review of the National Insurance Scheme in 1954. These endorsed the broad structure of the services, although they did point to future problems in funding pensions and in the NHS. They were accepted by the government. Full commitment to state welfare was only achieved in the late 1950s with the departure of Churchill in 1955 and the accession of Macmillan in 1957. Under Thorneycroft's Chancellorship (1955–7) spending on social services was held back to a growth rate of less than 1 per cent a year. A strong strand in Conservative politics maintained an opposition to collective social policies, typified in Powell and Macleod's attack on the cost of social services (1952). This re-echoes Churchill's original criticisms of Beveridge in 1942.

The theory of post-war consensus rests on the assertion of a continuity in policy bridging the 1951 change of government. The Conservative acceptance of the major reports on welfare issues has already been mentioned. However, there were four main discontinuities in policy between the 1945–51 and 1951–64 governments: in housing, social security, NHS and education policy. In the two former areas these were providing the basis for bitter political dispute by the late 1950s.

The change of government marked a progressive shift in housing policy from municipal provision to support for owner-occupation achieved mainly through the release of building materials to the private sector. About two million private sector and two and a half million public sector houses were built over the period, private sector construction outstripping the public sector in 1960. Support for private property is also evident in the 1957 de-control of much of the private rented sector and it was over this issue that the bitterest of controversy took place in the run-up to the 1959 election. However, by 1964 one family in four lived in a house built since 1951 and against this achievement, Labour's attacks gained little.

The issue of pension reform received continuous attention from both parties because the benefit was so low that about a quarter of recipients were also entitled to means-tested National Assistance throughout this period. A steady increase in the numbers of retired from about 1.8 million in 1951 to about 2.4 million in 1965, put an additional strain on the finances of the scheme. The scandal of non-take-up of means-tested supplementation was not officially quantified until 1966 (Ministry of Pensions and National Insurance, 1966) although it must have increased the hardship of pensioners substantially. The Labour party's National Superannuation scheme of 1957 proposed earnings-related pensions equivalent to half-pay for the entire workforce. The Conservative response was to increase pensions by 22 per cent in real terms in 1958 (the largest increase in the post-war period) and introduces a stop-gap earnings-related scheme in 1961. The real purchasing power of pensions in fact increased by just over 50 per cent over the life of the government, but pensions remained a major political issue throughout the next decade.

In the areas of the NHS and education, the discontinuities in policy were marked by substantial real expansions in spending on health service personnel and on providing schooling for the one and a half million extra pupils of the 'bulge' years. However, the large prescription and health charge increases of 1953 provoked Labour attacks (although Labour had itself introduced such charges in 1950). In secondary education, the failure to provide technical schools effectively reduced tripartition to grammar school/secondary modern bipartition, although the class division of selectivity did not become a major policy issue until the late 1960s.

This brief review indicates that if there was a substantial measure of political consensus on the foundation of the welfare state, consensus was something that contained real political conflicts. It had to be continually nurtured and renewed. A second strand to the consensus approach points the contrast between the post-war consensus and the mounting conflict of later years. How adequate is the perspective that charts out a voyage from agreement to controversy as the continuing story of the welfare state?

From consensus to conflict: political controversy from the 1960s onwards

The infection of conflict took place on two levels: theoretical and political. On the theoretical level the orthodoxy of welfare statism has been increasingly challenged. The blunt confrontation of official monetarism, summed up in the statement that 'public expenditure is at the heart of Britain's economic difficulties' in the opening sentence of the 1979 public expenditure white paper (Cmnd 7746, 1979, p. 1) provides a threat to the maintenance of social policy that needs no elaboration. There are many other challenges: Bacon and Eltis's thesis that the growth of the state sector hamstrings private industry by pre-empting the resource of skilled labour and directing it to areas where it cannot help production is well known (1976). Both Walker (1982, p. 11) and Gough (1979, p. 106) suggest that the argument may have influenced the thinking of the 1974–9 Labour government. In addition, the level of return from the welfare state is called into question. Hadley and Hatch summarise the case that increased investment in state welfare over the post-war period has not brought commensurate returns by any standards (1981, p. 55) and similar arguments are available elsewhere (Donnison, 1979; Pinker, 1979; MacGregor, 1981; Judge, 1982). However, theorising is not the best guide to the direction of policy.

Political controversy on welfare issues has certainly gained in intensity in recent years. In the area of secondary schooling, the 1964–70 Labour government encouraged comprehensive reform in a circular in 1965 and by 1970 was threatening legislation to enforce the system. The legislation was lost with the election, but the 1965 circular was immediately withdrawn in 1970. An Act making the comprehensive system compulsory was passed in 1976, to be repealed in turn in 1980. In the area of private schooling, Labour's commission of enquiry, set up in 1965 with terms of reference 'to advise on the best way of integrating public schools within the state system of education', points in a direction entirely opposite to the 1981 Assisted Places Scheme. Party approaches to council housing chart a similar course of developing party conflict. In the early 1950s Macmillan, as housing minister, was vying with the Labour post-war building levels. The 1972 Conservative Housing Finance Act proposed sharp rent increases and a phasing out of central government subsidies. The 1974 Labour response was a twelve-month rent freeze and a restriction on rent rises thereafter. The 1979 Conservative government had imposed a 53 per cent rent increase in real terms by the 1983 election and had sold off about one in thirteen council houses. The issue of rent control and security of tenure in the private sector provoked further conflict. The 1957 legislation decontrolled a quarter of a million private tenants and allowed increases for the remaining four and a half million. Labour legislation in 1965 provided mechanism for restricting the level of increases more closely. The introduction of shorthold tenure in 1981 provides for a completely decontrolled system of tenure.

Social security policy has been another area of contention. The debate over pensions in the late 1950s mentioned earlier extended into the 1964 and 1966 election campaigns where Labour's schemes formed a major plank in its manifesto. By 1969 a detailed White Paper was produced, but the legislation became bogged down in negotiations with the pension industry and was lost in the election. A radically different scheme was proposed by Conservatives in 1971, relying much more heavily on occupational provision. A modified version of the Labour scheme passed into law in 1975. One item in this – the mandatory link between pension-rates and wage-indices if these rise faster than price-indices – has already been abolished, and the future of pensions is under review in the Family Policy Group studies of February 1983. Policies on child support also differ: Labour increased universal family allowance in 1967 and 1968 by a substantial amount. The Conservative government introduced a new means-tested benefit (Family Income Supplement in 1971), probably as part of a strategy to expand the role of income-related social security radically in the Tax Credit Scheme set out in the 1972 Green Paper (Cmnd 5116). However, the Labour policy of integrating family allowances and child tax allowances as child benefits in 1976 was not opposed, and child benefits have been uprated to retain their purchasing power over the life of the 1979–83 government. The expansion of occupational sick-pay through the statutory sickness insurance scheme does represent a new departure in policy and one that has been strongly resisted by the Labour party. It has been suggested that this scheme foreshadows further privatisation of social security (Bull and Wilding, 1983, pp. 76–7).

Additional evidence of political conflict may be found in the abolition of earnings-related short-term benefits in 1981, the introduction of taxation of such benefits in 1983, the dilution of the Employment Protection Legislation of the mid-1970s by the 1980 Employment Act, the reintroduction of tax relief on employers health insurance contributions (abolished under the previous Labour government), the removal of compulsory national standards of school meal provision, and the support for the privatisation of a whole range of government services ranging from direct works council house building and maintenance to hospital ancillary services. All of these policies have generated vigorous political controversies in the early 1980s.

The evidence given here details some aspects of the growing intensity of party debates over welfare of recent years. It suggests a climate of increasing political controversy, rather than a transition from a politics of consensus to one of conflict in the area of welfare. How far is this view supported by the actual development of policy itself?

Continuities in the welfare state

In earlier sections, we questioned the extent of cosy consensus in the immediate post-war period. Political rhetoric must be distinguished from the facts of policy. Here we consider the development of policy from the 1950s to the 1980s, to explore how far the picture of mounting political conflict is supported by the facts.

In the major areas of state policy it is the continuities in policy rather than the departures of new administrations that provide the dominant theme. We review briefly the issues detailed above. In schooling, the controversies of the late 1960s and 1970s appear to have done little to affect the steady expansion of comprehensive schooling. Official statistics show a growth from about 10 per cent of the school population in 1965 to about 85 per cent by 1983. The opposition of the Conservative government of the early 1970s appears to have achieved little more than the retention of a small number of state selective schools alongside comprehensives in some areas. This of course undermines the comprehensive principle. However, the change in schooling practice has not resulted in a change in education in any extent commensurate with the difference in organisation. The authoritative National Children's Bureau study demonstrated that the proportion of middle-class children in secondary moderns and comprehensives was almost identical by 1974 (Steedman, 1980). Similarly the recommendations of the Public School Commissions actually resulted in rather more official encouragement of the practice whereby local authorities pay private sector fees for selected pupils and, in the mid-1970s, the abolition of the direct grant to an elite group of state schools. Most of these joined the private sector. The net result of this Labour attack on privilege was, paradoxically, to further strengthen exclusive education.

The struggles over the role of council housing represent a real issue. Yet they should not obscure the real Labour commitment to owner-occupation. The 1964 Labour government did not reverse the previous government's abolition of tax on the assumed rental value of an owned home (in 1963). Neither did it attack the system of mortgage relief, although in 1975 a ceiling was placed on the size of the mortgage which could command relief at a level of more than three times the mortgage which an average earner might obtain. The 1964–70 government, which achieved the highest house-building figures of the post-war years, was remarkably even-handed between private and public sector construction, averaging a little under two hundred thousand completions in each area annually over its lifetime. The 50 per cent decline in council house subsidies between 1979 and 1983 follows on a 30 per cent decline between 1974 and 1979. Gough characterises the distinctive features of 1979 Conservative policy aptly as 'more (or rather less) of the same' (1980, p. 9). It is in the scale of rent increases and subsidy cuts and in the policies of council house sales and towards the private sector that the Conservative government stands out. In the last-mentioned area, the failure to achieve large numbers of short-hold tenancies suggests that this departure does not merit too much attention.

Social security policies also betray more continuity than rhetoric might suggest. The pension schemes put forward by Labour underwent considerable dilution of their redistributive impact and modification to accommodate the private sector between 1957 and 1975. The ceiling for the earnings-related contribution was lowered from four times national average earnings to one and a half times – so that the highest paid would contribute roughly the same as skilled manual workers. In addition the Treasury subvention to the scheme, which was derived from a potentially more progressive system of taxation was reduced by about a third. Occupational schemes extracted two important concessions: those covered by such schemes were to be permitted to contract out of a third of contributions and some benefits from the state schemes. The state scheme also undertook to provide full cover for wives and widows of occupational pensioners, and to provide for the inflation proofing of both state and private components of the pension. This final concession removed a lot of the uncertainty from actuarial calculation in a period of high inflation and could result in a commitment to very large subsidies. Thus Labour accommodated the expansion of occupational pensions from about a quarter of the workforce in 1950 to about two-thirds in 1980. The expansion of means-testing has continued under both Labour and Conservative governments. The substantial increases in last resort benefits with the introduction of supplementary benefit in 1966 made large numbers of pensioners eligible for this benefit for the first time. The numbers claiming supplementary benefit have risen steadily through the 1970s from about three million in 1971 to four million by 1983, and the increase in dependence on this benefit among the long-term unemployed has extended under both Conservative and Labour governments.

Unless there are radical changes in policy, government support for private sector schemes in health care, education and elsewhere is unlikely to be sufficiently far-reaching to have much impact on the overall picture. Table 8 charts the picture of the steady expansion of private sector welfare over the post-war period. It can be seen that in most areas, particularly the two most important in terms of the amounts of money involved – housing and occupational pensions – the trend has been one of expansion. Uncertainty over the Labour government proposals may have played a part in delaying pension growth in the late 1960s, and the policies of Labour in the 1970s certainly acted as a barrier to private health care. The decline of private schooling does not seem to be linked to any government, and probably follows from the real increases in fees.

Overall there are real differences between the policies of different governments. However, these differences are less striking than the continuities. These continuities express the principles

TABLE 8
The growth of private welfare in the UK 1951–82

	1951	1956	1961	1966	1971	1976	1980	1982
Percentage of the labour force in occupational pension schemes:								
Men	30	39	50	62	55	65	68	NA
Women	12	19	25	26	34	50	55	NA
Percentage of the labour force in occupational sick pay schemes:								
Men	NA	NA	57	⎰NA	71	77	84	NA
Women	NA	NA		⎱NA	71	80	84	NA
Percentage of housing:								
Owned	31	35	39	45	50	53	55	59
Rented from local authorities	17	22	27	29	31	32	32	30
Rented privately	52	43	33	26	19	15	13	11
Percentage of pupils in independent schools:								
	5.0	6.2	7.7	7.2	6.1	5.6	5.8	5.9
Percentage of population covered by private health insurance:								
	0.2	1.4	2.1	3.0	3.8	3.9	6.1	7.7

Sources:

Pensions: *Social Trends*, no. 12 and *Sixth Survey of Occupational Pension Schemes*, Government Actuary, 1981, Table 2:3.
Sick pay: *Social Trends*, no. 12, p. 70 and *Occupational Sick Pay*, Cmnd 7864, 1980, p. 18.
Housing: *Social Trends*, no. 12, p. 149 and *Social Trends*, no. 14, p. 117.
Education: *Social Trends*, no. 14, Table 3:2.
Health care: *Social Trends*, no. 14, p. 111 and Table 1:2 and A. Seldon, *Wither the Welfare State*, IEA, 1982, p. 56.

that have underlain the development of welfare policy.

The rigidities of the welfare state

To begin at the Beveridge, the three features of new right 'innovation' identified in chapter 1 are clearly evident throughout social policy. Beveridge's third guiding principle for social security encapsulates a distinction between deserving and undeserving groups, support for the private sector and the assumption of family dependency;

The third principle is that social security must be achieved by co-operation between the state and the individual. The state should offer security for service and contribution. The state in organising security should not stifle incentive, opportunity, responsibility; in establishing a national minimum, it should leave room and encouragement for voluntary action by each individual to provide more than that minimum for himself and his family (1942, p. 7).

The principle of security 'for service and contribution' effectively distinguishes favoured and unfavoured groups. Flat rate benefits adequate to meet the contingencies of everyday life were to be provided to members of the insurance scheme. The feckless minority outside the world of steady employment and the work ethic would be dependent on means-tested assistance. This would be subject to rigorous testing and also 'to any conditions as to behaviour which may seem likely to hasten restoration of earning capacity' (p. 141). The issue of maintenance of work-ethic also led to the establishment of a test of availability for work in the administration of unemployment benefit. Part of the case for universal family allowance was also based on a similar consideration: if such allowances were not paid to those in work, subsistence benefit for large families out of work might exceed wage levels and this was judged 'dangerous' (p. 154).

The development of the social security system resulted in a deeper entrenchment of a division of claimants. The most important factors were two: first, the decision to 'blanket in' most of the elderly in 1948 at relatively low rates of insurance pension, so that it became difficult to raise insurance benefits above subsistence levels. This led Beveridge himself to repudiate policy in 1953: 'either the government will have to raise the benefit rates to adequacy . . . or to say . . . that they have formally abandoned security against want without a means-test and declare that they drop the Beveridge report . . .' (Hansard, House of Lords, vol. 182, col. 677). This issue led to the proposals for earnings-related pensions, and the final enactment of such schemes in 1975. However, the long introduction period of the scheme means that many pensioners will be dependent on means-tested supplementation until the 1990s.

Secondly, official decisions to reduce the rate of family allowance and to restrict the length of unemployment insurance in the implementation of Beveridge subjected further groups to means-testing. To the stigma of the income test has been added the misery of the division between long-term and short-term Supplementary Benefit rates in 1971 which widens the gulf between deserving and undeserving recipients. The continued increase in the number of unemployed dependent on means-tested welfare to about two-thirds of this group by 1981 as the average length of unemployment lengthens, has led a recent commentator to describe means-tested welfare as assuming a 'mass role' (Fimister, 1983, p. 28).

Beveridge expressed strong support for a private sector operating in tandem with the state:

> in so far as voluntary insurance meets real needs, it is an essential part of security; scope and encouragement for it must be provided. The state can ensure this negativity . . . by limiting benefits to subsistence and primary needs and . . . positively by regulation, by financial assistance or by itself undertaking the organisation of voluntary insurance.

The steady expansion of private pension schemes mainly run by employers and subsidised and to some extent regulated by government is in turn with this development. The issue of the scope left for private pensions in state schemes has been one of the major problems in all pension proposals since the mid-1960s (Kincaid, 1975, ch. 8; Room, 1979, pp. 85–8; Fogarty, 1983, p. 254).

Beveridge's assumption of the family dependency of married women as justifying lower benefits (sick and unemployment benefits at 80 per cent of the single person's level, and a 'half-test' for any pension entitlement at all) and a contracting out option for them and a higher rate of contribution for men paying in for the couple 'as a team' has already been mentioned. The reforms of the mid-1970s and early 1980s bring married women closer to full participation in the scheme, although the rights to dependant's benefits are still inferior to those of men. The basic 'liable relative' rule of social assistance, where cohabiting couples are treated as husband and wife, still assumes houshold dependency. Beveridge's original separation and divorce benefits for women were removed from the scheme to cut costs. This resulted in the dependence on means-tested benefits of an important group of lone parents. The assumption of family dependence and care is also apparent in the rules governing the new Invalid Care Allowance which is simply not available to married women caring for a relative and in the Non-Contributory Invalidity Pension, which defines married women's entitlement in terms of inability to carry out household tasks. This is a much stricter test than incapacity for paid work which is the rule applied to men (Land, 1978).

In the area of education, some of the most far-reaching changes in the scope and organisation of policy have taken place. The minimum period of schooling has been extended from 9 to 11 years and the use of higher education has more than doubled (Halsey et al., 1980, p. 188). The principle of comprehensive provision for the mass of secondary school pupils has been accepted. The examination system has been expanded so that over three-quarters of school-leavers had no qualification in the immediate post-war years, as compared with 14 per cent in 1981 (Halsey et al., 1980, p. 109, and DES Statistical Bulletin 11/83, Table 2). However, the continuities in provision remain powerful and consistent throughout the period. The study undertaken by Halsey and his colleagues provides the most comprehensive analysis of the effect of the post-war changes on class differences in educational opportunity. The chances of working-class children attending selective secondary schools in the 1950s and 1960s are shown to be roughly the same as those in the 1920s and actually less than those in the 1930s. The fall in opportunity is roughly uniform across classes and may be accounted for in demographic terms: there were relatively fewer selective places for the increased population of post-war years. The educational reforms had very little effect on class differences in access to selective schooling (Halsey et al., 1980, p. 63).

Halsey's study deals with children entering secondary school before 1964. The data from the National Children's Bureau study presented in the previous section indicates that class differences still persist within the comprehensive system. If a different measure of success within the system, examination achievement, is used, Halsey's data demonstrates a continuing disadvantage in the opportunity for working class children to stay on at school beyond the minimum school leaving age (p. 140) and to succeed in gaining advanced examination successes (see also Reid, 1977, pp. 186–7). The influence of parental occupation on success within comprehensive schools is also reported in more recent work (Rutter et al., 1979, p. 87; Neave, 1975).

Considerable changes have also been made in the treatment of women in schools. The Sex Discrimination Act of 1975 was applied to mixed sex schools and it is clear from a comparison of the situation revealed by a survey by the Inspectorate in that year and more recent evidence that considerable advances have been made in equalising the availability of different subjects to girls and boys (Reid and Wormald, 1982, pp. 99–104). This may contribute to the long-term trend of convergence in the rates for staying on at school and gaining passes in advanced examinations with both 17 per cent of girls and boys gaining at least one A-level by 1981 (DES, Statistical Bulletin 11/83). However, this change may be limited in its effect. The differential tendency for boys to take A-levels in the science and technology subjects which are most likely to lead to careers and to pursue career-orientated higher and further education is as marked as in earlier years (Reid and Wormald, 1982, pp. 90–1). The influence of the 'hidden curriculum' (Deem, 1981, p. 136) and of wider social pressures (McRobbie, 1978) in socialising girls into particular social pathways is as strong as ever.

The paradoxical results of the attempts to limit the influence of the private sector which resulted from the Public Schools Commission Reports of 1968 and 1970 were reviewed in the preceding section. The pattern of education indicates that patterns of class and gender privilege are firmly entrenched in the system, despite the limited gains in the education of women and in the development of comprehensive schooling that have been made.

The National Health Service has been described as the 'most socialist of the social services' (Navarro, 1980, p. 1). The achievement of providing health care for all, free (more or less) at the point of use, should not be underestimated. However, recent research, summarised in the Black Report (1982), indicates that class differentials in health standards persist throughout the period. By some measures they increase. Townsend writes in an edited version of the report: 'during the twenty years up to the early 1970s . . . the mortality rates for both men and women aged thirty-five and over in occupational classes I and II have steadily diminished, while those in IV and V changed very little or even deteriorated' (Townsend and Davidson, 1982, p. 15). A similar picture emerges if other indications of health standards, such as absence from work through illness, self-report of poor health or the use of GP or of hospital services are employed (pp. 72–3, 77–81). The conclusion of a review of explanations of the continuing link between social class and health point to the limited scope of the service: it is factors beyond its control 'in terms of the more diffuse consequences of the class structure: poverty, work conditions . . . and deprivation . . . in the home and its immediate environment, at work, in education and the upbringing of children and more generally in family and social life' that are important (p. 134).

The trends in inequality between men and women are complex. Male mortality rates are higher than women's in every social class. In recent years the gap has tended to widen (Townsend and

Davidson, 1982, p. 74). The use of other measures produces a rather different picture. Women report more feelings of ill-health than men, consult GPs and visit hospitals more frequently and are incapable of work through illness more often (Reid and Wormald, 1982, pp. 34–48). The gender issue in health care that has attracted most attention in recent years concerns provision for dependency groups. The policy of 'community care' has gained support from both political parties throughout the post-war period (Walker, 1983, p. 159). It is a gender issue because, as Ungerson points out, women are both the chief providers and chief recipients of unpaid care in the community (1982, p. 1). The principle of extending care in the community was firmly laid out in the 1963 Ministry of Health Report: Health and Welfare (Cmnd 1973). This covered four groups: the elderly, the mentally ill and the physically and mentally handicapped. The motives behind the expansion of community care were twofold. On the one hand a number of reports (for example Townsend, 1965) traced the problems of institutionalisation. On the other it was necessary to reduce the cost of replacing the large number of obsolete hospitals and homes built in the Victorian period (Walker, 1983, p. 159).

The problems of community care are highlighted by two factors. The aims of policy in shifting resources away from residential provision towards support for community care have not been met. In fact the proportion of Local Authority personal services expenditure going on community care actually fell by 13 per cent over the period 1974 to 1981 (Walker, 1982, p. 21) whereas that directed to residential care increased. In addition the demands made on carers have risen. More married women are in paid employment and there are relatively more frail elderly people requiring care. In this context, the evidence of discrimination between men and women in the provision of support services for carers of relatives in the community is an indication of continuing gender discrimination (Kahn and Kamerman, 1978, p. 342; Ungerson, 1982, p. 38).

Although more attention has been paid to the impact of community care in recent years, it is a policy that dates back to the early 1960s. Moreover, the assumption on which it is based – that married women are available in the community to provide care because their role as dependants of male breadwinners supports them in unpaid care-work – is evident in policy throughout the post-war history of the welfare state. The problems of community care do not arise from new departures but from a historical consistency.

The brief review of evidence on the development of major social services in this section indicates that, despite the substantial changes of the post-war period, underlying principles of support for the private sector, social division in policy and a distinct status for women have been a consistent feature of the practice of the welfare state. It is important not to minimise the increase in standards of social welfare that resulted from the post-war reforms. In particular, the establishment of the NHS achieved an immeasurable improvement in access to health care for working-class women (Thane, 1982, p. 236), the Beveridge scheme extended unemployment and retirement benefits, the housing programme resulted in a marked rise in working-class living standards and the extension of education raised the level of schooling. However, it is not clear that the principles often associated with the new right were absent at the inception of the modern welfare state, nor that they were uninfluential throughout its history. If this is the case, the view that the welfare state is currently undergoing radical change as a result of a new right incursion is undermined. This is the theme of the next chapter.

4

Current developments in the welfare state

No-one can seriously deny that, whatever else Thatcherism represents, it embodies a genuine ideological break with the social democratic post-war consensus.

Phil Lee, *Marxism Today*, May 1983

The Conservative Policy is simply more (or rather less) of the same.

Ian Gough, *Marxism Today*, July 1980

The third aspect of new crisis theory discussed in chapter 1 was the claim that welfare policy suffered an abrupt reversal in the late 1970s. A watershed was crossed in the long march from 1944. Public opinion shifted to the right. In this chapter we consider how far current developments measure up to such apocalyptic rhetoric. The terrain is divided up into the areas of cuts, privatisation and the impact on women discussed in chapter 1.

The cuts and restructuring

Current changes in social spending have been discussed along two dimensions – cuts and restructuring. Both changes reach across the electoral boundaries of Labour and Conservative governments.

The idea of welfare cuts has been prominent in the rhetoric of politicians since the sterling crisis of 1975, when Crosland informed local authorities that 'the party was over'. The following

TABLE 9
Public expenditure on the main social programmes 1978/9, 1983/4

(Billions of pounds at 1982/3 prices, deflated by the GDP total home costs deflator)

	1978–9	1979–80	1980–1	1981–2	1982–3	1983–4
Total social expenditure	57.2 (100%)	58.1 (101.6%)	58.8 (102.8%)	60 (104.9%)	61.7 (107.9%)	62.9 (110%)
Social security	26.7 (100%)	27.0 (101.1%)	27.5 (103%)	30.5 (114.2%)	32.5 (121.7%)	33.6 (125.8%)
Education	12.6 (100%)	12.4 (98.4%)	12.8 (101.6%)	12.6 (100%)	12.7 (100.8%)	12.7 (100.8%)
Health and personal social services	12.1 (100%)	12.4 (102.5%)	13.3 (109.9%)	13.6 (112.4%)	13.8 (114%)	14.0 (115.7%)
Housing	5.8 (100%)	6.3 (108.6%)	5.2 (89.7%)	3.3 (56.9%)	2.7 (46.6%)	2.6 (44.8%)
Social expenditure as a percentage of:						
public expenditure	53.5%	54.2%	54.1%	53.8%	54.4%	54.9%
Gross Domestic Product	21.7%	22%	23%	23.6%	23.7%	23.6%
Deflator (Index of total home costs)	63.3	71.6	85.3	93.9	100	105.1

Sources: *The Government's Expenditure Plans, 1984–5 to 1986–7* (Cmnd 9143, 1984), Table 1:14. *National Income and Expenditure* (CSO, 1983), Table 1:1 and 2:5.

year, the prime minister assured the party conference 'we used to think you could spend your way out of . . . a recession . . . I tell you in all candour that option no longer exists.' However, expenditure reductions are not so dramatic as these phrases imply. A convenient approach to social spending is to consider the proportion of Gross Domestic Product spent on the five major social services (social security, the NHS, council housing, education and the personal social services). This has remained roughly constant since the late 1970s at between 24 and 26 per cent of GDP. Some of the increase in the ratio between 1979–80 and 1980–1 is accounted for by the 2 per cent fall in GDP between those years, but this does not apply to subsequent years. This overall stability conceals changes in the cost of different programmes. Expenditure on education, health care and personal social services has changed little whereas that on social security has increased rapidly and that on local authority housing has fallen and is now at less than half the level of the mid-1970s (Table 9).

The cost of social security has risen for two reasons: most importantly the rise in the number of unemployed from about one million in 1975 to over three million by 1983 fuels demand for benefits. However, the gradual improvements in pensions following the 1975 Social Security Act and the increase in numbers of retirement pensioners (from just under eight and a half to just over nine million over the period) due to demographic trends and a tendency to retire earlier in recession also play a part. Within this total there have been divergences between the programmes for different groups. By 1983 cuts in the real value of child benefit, pension and unemployment benefit increases had been restored. However the decision to abolish the earnings-related supplement for short-term benefits (mainly for the unemployed), the cut in these benefits to take account of their inclusion in the income tax net, and the failure to increase levels at a faster rate than price indices have meant that the living standards of the unemployed fell relative to those of the rest of the population. The cuts in school-meal provision in some education authorities, increases in council house rents and the decision to substantially reduce levels of housing benefit in April 1984 are also likely to bear most heavily in this group. These cuts divide the unemployed minority from the employed majority, although they do not involve very large amounts of state spending.

Housing cuts have resulted in a decline in local authority completions from over 130,000 in 1976 to under 40,000 in 1982 and rent rises in real terms of just over 70 per cent over that period (Cmnd 8494, vol. II, p. 29). The fact that expenditure on health care, education and personal social services has not changed dramatically over the period does not mean that needs are satisfactorily met: the increase in numbers of elderly, the real pay rises achieved by personnel in the early 1970s and the severe cuts in capital spending result in increased pressure on the NHS. The health service spends, on average, about two and a half times as much per head on people over sixty-five as on those between five and sixty-five; and numbers over sixty-five increased by about 3 per cent from 1976 to 1982 (CSO, 1983, pp. 19 and 115). In education, provision for under-fives is contracting and the opportunities to improve pupil/teacher ratios presented by the fall in the school age population (from 8.7 to 8.1 million over the period) have not been grasped. The Inspectorate's report on the effect of financial policies in 1982 implied with all the caution of an official document that cuts have damaged standards.

> it is difficult enough for educational policies . . . to be seen and developed . . . in educational terms and, in too many cases, financial mechanisms at least (and in some cases finance tout court) aggravate the problem. This year's report shows that the pace of deterioration in provision has at least been slowed . . . (Department of Education and Science, 1983, p. 32).

However, the same report states that 'the great majority of education in schools and colleges is adequately provided for' (p. 6). The deficiencies bear as in many other areas of policy disproportionately on the least privileged groups.

In addition, the fact that education, housing and personal social services are provided by local government which has a measure of autonomy in the implementation of central government plans results in variations between areas. Some authorities have attempted to resist rent increases, whereas others have abandoned school-meals services and pre-school provision entirely. Attempts by central government to shift the burden of a policy of expenditure constraint on to local authorities have resulted in a series of measures to cut local spending, including reductions in the Rate Support Grant. These have not been successful in cutting local spending, although the proportion of that spending financed by rates had risen from 24 to 36 per cent between 1976 and 1983 (CSO, 1983, p. 96). The 1984 Rates Act may succeed in imposing cuts by undermining local government powers to determine rates. However Conservative opposition is likely to dilute this measure in practice.

The argument that the gross facts of public expenditure

represent a new departure in social policy stands out in relief once comparisons are made over the long term. Such comparisons must necessarily be crude, due to the problems of differences in official calculation, changes in Treasury control of spending departments, changes in need and in demand, and changes in what given quantities of money will buy, in personnel and materials. However certain general judgments may be made.

State expenditure has grown steadily as a proportion of GDP from about a third in 1950 to about 45 per cent in the mid-1970s. Since then there has been a slight fall (Gould and Roweth, 1980, p. 343; Sleeman, 1979, pp. 51–7; Walker (ed.), 1982, p. 7; Gough, 1979, pp. 84–101; Berthoud et al. 1981, ch. 1). The growth of expenditure over the period is neither particularly rapid, compared to that in other advanced countries (Rose and Peters, 1978; Gough, 1979, p. 79), nor has it achieved unusually high levels (Walker (ed.), 1982, p. 7; Gough, 1979, p. 78; OECD, 1984, p. 6).

Public expenditure through most of the post-war period shows a pattern of steady growth at an annual average rate of just over 3 per cent a year. This overall pattern is interrupted by sharper rates of growth in the early 1950s, in 1967 and 1974, succeeded by cutbacks. The post-1975 reductions in expenditure represent a new era of stabilisation. Annual growth rates over the period of the 1974–9 Labour government fell to about 1.5 per cent, and over the 1979–83 Conservative government to about half a per cent (Bull and Wilding, 1983, p. 23). The long-term increase has been fuelled by a substantial real rise in taxation (Judge, 1982).

Social spending shows rather a different pattern. The rate of increase exceeded that of public expenditure as a whole, moving ahead in the early 1960s and expanding even more rapidly in the 1970s. Relative expansion continues in the early 1980s despite attempts at restraint. Social expenditure in fact accounts for about three-quarters of the growth in public spending over the period from 1951 to 1983 (Judge, 1982, p. 29). The major area of cutback which has enabled this expansion has been defence spending. This has grown at less than 1 per cent a year over the period, compared to a social spending increase approaching 5 per cent, and a total public expenditure increase of slightly more than 3 per cent. It is at present unclear whether the very large increases in defence budgets since 1979 and attempts to cut social spending constitute a reversal of the trends. The most recent official plans talk only of reducing the growth in spending to a 'modest' rate of increase (Treasury, 1984, p. 20).

The impact of constraint since the mid-1970s has been to achieve a fresh stabilisation of expenditure. From this perspective, the new departure in social expenditure may be represented as a real change. However, the change is one of containment of increases rather than cuts. Despite the regretful pronouncements of Labour politicians and the more enthusiastic rhetoric of the 1979 and 1983 governments, substantial real cuts in welfare spending have not been realised (the sole exception being council house building). Table 10 shows annual rates of increase in spending under Labour and Conservative governments since the war. The pattern is clearly complex. There do not appear to be real reductions since 1979, except in the areas of education (where the numbers of children in school have fallen) and in housing where house building has borne the brunt of the slow-down in the increase in social spending.

For the reason that cuts do not form a simple pattern, most commentators on changes in the welfare state combine analysis of the cuts with accounts of restructuring. These have been developed in several directions. Gough analyses changes in terms of denationalisation, increases in consumer charges and a deliberate attack on trade unions and the organisation of the working class through encouragement of individual work incentives and the division of stereotyped deserving and undeserving groups. Feminists argue that current policy attempts to reinforce the oppression of women through the weakening of sex discrimination and employment protection legislation, and the extension of

TABLE 10
Patterns of social expenditure under Conservative and Labour governments: annual changes 1950–85 (%)

	Conservative	Labour	Conservative	Labour	Conservative	Average
	1950–64	1964–70	1970–74	1974–79	1979–84	1950–84
Total social expenditure	4.2	5.9	6.8	2.0	1.7	4.1
Social security	4.9	6.5	3.1	5.9	4.9	5.1
Education	5.6	5.5	4.0	0.4	0.5	3.9
Health and personal social services	3.1	6.2	7.1	2.9	2.6	4.0
Housing	2.5	4.0	19.9	−7.0	−11.7	1.3

Note: 1979–84 figures are calculated from the same source as Table 9.

Sources: K. Judge in A. Walker, 1982, Table 2:2 and HM Treasury, *The Government's Expenditure Plans 1984–5 to 1986–7* (Cmnd 9143), 1984.

community care and family-based welfare policies. This is considered in detail in a separate section. Other writers have emphasised the racist and nationalist elements of policy (for example, Barker, 1980; Birmingham Centre for Contemporary Cultural Studies, 1982). From the point of view of welfare politics, institutionalised racism is most apparent in the introduction of citizenship requirements for free NHS treatment and in the withdrawal of support from urban aid and education programmes for ethnic minorities as a result of expenditure constraint. Racism in areas such as housing allocation had been an endemic feature of social policy preceding current developments (Karn, 1981).

The most important aspect of government policy which affects working-class organisation is undoubtedly unemployment. Unemployment has increased sharply from about half a million in 1974 to over 3 million by July 1983. About 800 thousand of the extra 2.7 million had joined the registers by 1979 and nearly 2 million after the election of the Conservative government (Table 11).

The issue of how far this increase can be attributed to government policy is hotly disputed. Metcalfe suggests that two long-run factors outside the control of government have played a part. These are the decline in employment in manufacturing, mining and construction industries (which have lost over 4 million

TABLE 11
Unemployment: numbers and rates, 1974–1983

	Number (millions):			Percentage of economically active population:		
	Men	*Women*	*Total*	*Men*	*Women*	*Overall*
1974	0.5	0.1	0.6	3.4	1.3	2.6
1975	0.8	0.2	1.0	5.5	2.1	4.1
1976	1.0	0.3	1.4	7.1	3.5	5.7
1977 (a)	1.0	0.4	1.4	7.3	3.7	5.8
1978	1.0	0.4	1.4	7.0	3.8	5.7
1979	0.9	0.4	1.3	6.5	3.7	5.3
1980	1.2	0.5	1.7	8.3	4.8	6.8
1981	1.8	0.7	2.5	13.0	6.9	10.5
1982	2.1	0.8	2.9	15.2	8.0	12.2
1983	2.2	0.9	3.1	15.8	9.0	13.0

Note: (a) Figures after 1977 are calculated on the new basis of benefit claimants only; this reduces the total by at least 10 per cent.

Sources: *Department of Employment Gazettes*: January 1984, Table 2:1 and October 1980, Table 2:1; *Social Trends*, no. 9, Table 5:12.

jobs since 1966) and the real increase in the return to labour in recent years. This results in large part from the spread of unionisation. In addition the sharp rise in oil prices from 1974 onwards and the general worsening in terms of trade have played a lesser role (Metcalfe in Coppock and Prest, 1982, p. 264). Calculations by Nickell on this basis attribute just under half of unemployment in 1978 to these factors (Layard, Metcalfe and Nickell, 1979). This suggests that responsibility for more than half the unemployment of the early 1980s may be laid at the door of the government.

A similar claim is outlined in more guarded language in the report of the House of Commons Treasury and Civil Service Committee published just before the 1983 election. This criticised estimates of future unemployment rates and economic growth contained in the 1983 budget and argued for stronger state intervention to bring down interest rates. It also claimed that the 'overall balance between expenditure on current consumption and investment . . . is wrong' (HCP 286, 1983, p. XVII). This implies support for the view that better economic performance and lower unemployment could be achieved by different government pol-icies.

Unemployment as a social policy drives a wedge between the majority of the working class in work (who have achieved real rises in living standards in recent years) and the minority of the unemployed. The increase in the average earnings index of nearly 70 per cent between 1979 and 1983 comfortably outstrips the retail price index increase of 51 per cent (Department of Employment, September 1983). For those out of work benefits have kept pace with prices but not with earnings. The brutal fact is that since 1976 the value of unemployment benefit for a married couple has fallen from about half to about a third of average earnings (CSO, 1984, p. 76). The increase in long-term unemployment (by 1981 more than a third of the unemployed had been out of work for more than a year – Department of Employment, September 1983) has led to a virtual breakdown of the national insurance system for the unemployed. Among male claimants (no figures are available for women) the numbers receiving national insurance benefit roughly equalled those dependent on means-tested supplementary benefit up to 1979. Since then the numbers on supplementary benefit have increased sharply to about double that of national insurance claimers in 1983 (CSO, 1984, p. 76). The decision to cut housing benefits from April 1984 will bear most heavily on this group.

In general the proportion of all social security expenditure going to the unemployed has risen from 8 to 17 per cent of the total between 1979 and 1983 (Social Security Advisory Committee, 1983, p. 6). This, plus the increase in the number of single-parent families dependent on means-tested benefits, accounts for virtually all the increase (from 28 to 38 per cent) of the proportion of social security expenditure going on non-contributory benefits.

The miseries of unemployment in a work-ethic society are well-documented (Sinfield, 1981, pp. 35–40). To these are added the harassment and insecurity of dependence on means-tested welfare (Bradshaw and Deacon, 1983, pp. 134–5) and the despair of living at a standard which steadily falls behind that of the working class in work. The division in the political strength of Labour resulting from the threat of joblessness, together with cuts in strikers' benefits and a series of legislative measures compelling private ballots and weakening links with the Labour party have tended to undermine trade unionism. Union membership fell from about 13.5 to about 12.2 million between 1979 and 1981, the sharpest fall since the 1920s (CSO, 1984, p. 155).

With the exception of council housing, there do not appear to be major cuts in social spending. The most important policy change of the late 1970s is the refusal of government to mitigate unemployment. This may weaken overall working-class organisation, but its central inhumanities are confined to a minority of the population. Bearing this in mind, we may assent to O'Higgins's conclusion:

> the examination . . . of expenditure plans and outcomes under the Conservative government suggests that beliefs that it would lead to radical changes . . . are so far unfounded, not so much because the government has changed its mind, but because it has been unable to implement its rhetoric (1983, p. 175).

The suggestion that the welfare state is currently being restructured rather than cut carries more force if policy analysis also considers tolerance of very high levels of unemployment. A further aspect of restructuring on market principles concerns the attempt to denationalise welfare.

Privatisation and charges

In these areas the policies of the 1979 government stand in sharp contrast with those of its predecessor. Council house rents, optical, dental and prescription charges, the cost of school meals and a range of personal social services charges have increased sharply. Because many of these charges are set by local authorities the scale of the increases and the standard of service provided varies. The policy of direct charging is often seen as complementary to denationalising welfare services, for two reasons. High direct charges make state provision less attractive. If a greater proportion of service costs are provided by charges to users rather than by compulsory taxation, the viability of transfer to the private sector is enhanced.

Manifesto promises to accelerate the sale of council housing, to subsidise the fees of selected independent school entrants, to bring back pay-beds to NHS hospitals and partially restore tax reliefs for private health insurance were kept in the first year of office (Conservative Party, 1979, pp. 23–7). Between 1979 and April 1983 about 475,000 houses were sold to sitting tenants by local authorities (Cmnd 8789, vol. II, p. 34). The assisted places scheme which subsidises fees at independent schools from 1981 onwards provides for about 5,500 entrants each year. Private health insurance has expanded rapidly. The number of people covered has increased by 68 per cent between the end of 1978 and the end of 1982 to reach a total of 4.2 million: just under half of subscribers to these schemes are members of employers' schemes, but it is in this sector that the most rapid expansion is taking place (CSO, 1984, p. 111).

The future scope of privatisation is unclear. Private health care accounted for only 6 per cent of all hospital beds in England in 1981. The overview of Provident Scheme statistics for that year reports underlying rates of growth showing significant reductions since the 'boom' year of 1980 and refers to 'growing pressure on operating margins' (BUPA, 1982, p. 6). By 1982 the increase in subscriptions had fallen to 3 per cent compared with 26 per cent in 1980 (CSO, 1984, p. 111).

Sales of local authority dwellings built up from about 80,000 in 1980 to 100,000 in 1981 and a peak of just over 200,000 in 1982. For the first two quarters of 1983 the figures have declined to under 80,000 (Department of the Environment, 1983, p. 16). Council house sales are predominantly in the preferred categories of semi-detached houses with gardens. Since only about a third of all council tenancies fall into this category, it is possible that current levels of sales will not be maintained (see Murie, 1981, p. 212). The level of discount on sales is now 43 per cent.

The annual surveys of independent schools carried out by the DES and by the Independent Schools Information Service both indicate that the independent sector reached a peak of about 6 per cent of the total school population in 1980. Since then numbers have declined at about 1 per cent a year in line with the fall in numbers of school-age children. Since independent schools recruit almost entirely from middle and upper class groups, and the birth rate among these groups has not fallen as fast as that for lower groups, independent schools may in fact be educating a smaller proportion of the social class from which they have traditionally drawn support (Independent Schools Information Service, 1983, p. 3). The assisted places scheme itself contributed to the fees of less than 3 per cent of independent school children in 1983. This should be contrasted with the continuing state subsidies from local education authorities (accounting for about 6 per cent) and from the armed forces and the diplomatic corps (accounting for about 12 per cent). These programmes have existed since the end of the Second World War. In fact the Independent Schools Information Service comments that the Assisted Places Scheme grants 'are to a large extent offset by a drop in assisted places being taken up by local authorities' (1983, p. 4). The new scheme has not substantially affected the scale of state subsidy to private education.

Other significant shifts of policy emphasis include changes in the death grant so that this is concentrated solely on the poor, with the implication that the rest of the population must insure privately to meet funeral expenses; and the introduction of a statutory sickness insurance scheme in 1983 whereby responsibility for income-maintenance during the first eight weeks of sickness passes from the national insurance scheme to private insurance organised by the employer. This is likely to increase employer surveillance of absence due to sickness as there is a direct interest in keeping this to a minimum.

The impact of these changes is also minor. Death grants at £20 in 1983 were so low as to be a minor contribution to funeral costs. Most employers operate schemes to top-up employees' state sick benefit. By the mid-1970s about 59 per cent of male and 55 per cent of female employees were covered by firms' schemes for the first eight weeks. Two-thirds of men and 85 per cent of women were entitled to full pay (or pay minus NI benefits) in these schemes (Cmnd 7864, 1980, Tables 4 and 5). The change is likely to constitute a division between those in such schemes and others who are forced to rely on the less satisfactory minimal cover under the new legislation, rather than a major change in the experience of sick benefit for most workers.

The development of privatisation is apparent in support for the contracting out of council house building and maintenance and hospital ancillary and domestic services. This has met with little success. Indeed between 1979 and 1981 the proportion of NHS expenditure on laundry going to outside contractors actually fell from 14.1 to 11.7 per cent and on domestic cleaning services from 2.4 to 2.1 per cent (NHS Unlimited, 1983, p. 5). In local government a Parliamentary Answer on 23 March 1984 showed that only 23 privatisation schemes worth an average of no more than £300,000 each had been put into practice. This indicates the problems experienced in obtaining satisfactory service from the private sector. The failure of privatisation policies probably underlies recent decisions to make some private services exempt from VAT and compel health authorities to obtain private tenders. Tenancy law has also been changed to introduce a new form of tenure – short-hold – with fewer rights to security or rent regulation. This has again led to the creation of far fewer new tenancies than was originally anticipated; only 3,500 short-hold tenancies were registered by August 1981 (Roof, 1983, p. 6).

It is perhaps in the area of policy discussion that enthusiasm for a shift to the private sector is most apparent. Leaked reports from the Central Policy Review Staff in September 1982 and the Family Policy Group in February 1983 discuss measures that would substantially change the welfare state: the introduction of private insurance funding for health care; vouchers in state education; real reduction in the major welfare benefits; and a greater reliance on the family for care. However, there is little indication that these plans will be put into practice. State funding for health care and the levels of the major welfare benefits have been maintained, voucher schemes are not available and the expansion of community care follows previous trends. While the political ideology of 'rolling back the frontiers of the state' is strongly evident, the practice of denationalisation in the welfare area is limited. Private welfare systems appear to be expanding in health care and education, but it seems likely that this trend will soon reach an upper limit.

State support for private welfare also throws a fresh perspective on arguments about cuts in state spending. Titmuss drew attention to the importance of fiscal policies and occupational benefits in people's overall welfare position in the mid-1950s. Writers in social policy have paid increasing attention to these issues in recent years (Field, 1981; Le Grand, 1982; Sinfield, 1978; Pond, 1982; Titmuss, 1962). It is argued that tax concessions and other forms of support for private welfare constitute covert subsidies. The expansion of private welfare has implications for state revenue forgone in such subsidies. The debate about whether tax allowances and reliefs can be thought of as subsidies is complex (Pond, 1982, pp. 59–60). Opponents of the notion argue that to think of the decision not to levy tax on a particular item as a subsidy is to embrace the idea that all income should be taxed by the state in the first place. This offends against the notion of freedom. However, this is to suggest that people's allocation of their own income is free from influence by the state so long as the state does not actually command that income through tax.

Tax concessions have considerable implications for the kind of choices people are likely to make, and must be taken into account in any discussion of how the state organises welfare.

From the 1979 public expenditure white paper (Cmnd 7439) onwards, the government has published annual estimates of the value of tax relief (Table 12). These are subject to wide margins of error, but give an indication of the levels of subsidy. The most striking increase is in subsidies to owner-occupiers, although this is particularly difficult to quantify, since some aspects of it only apply to some owners (for example mortgage interest relief).

Occupational pension provision also receives large and rapidly growing subsidies. It should be noted that the figure here does not include the exemption from capital gains tax of the proceeds of pension funds. Kincaid calculated the value of this as about one and a half times the Exchequer subsidy to the entire national insurance scheme in 1976 (1978, p. 370). The table gives the official estimates from the 1983 public expenditure white paper. These take into account the tax exemptions on employees' contributions and pension funds investment income. A recent Inland Revenue paper suggested that the tax-exempt status of lump sums paid on retirement by many schemes and the fact that a major component of pensions arises from employers' contributions which are tax-exempt should also enter the calculation (Inland Revenue, 1983). This produces a figure of just over double the one quoted. Table 12 provides a conservative estimate of this important tax subsidy.

The value of tax relief to employers on contributions made on behalf of employees to health care insurance schemes is not included in official statistics. The table gives the author's own estimates which are subject to a wide margin of error. Statistics published by the main private health insurance schemes give the value of such contributions. To these the average rate of corporation tax on net company profits assessed for such tax is applied. This assumes that this calculation of the rate of tax is appropriate and that companies who participate in such schemes pay average tax rates. The calculation indicates that subsidies in this area have risen substantially in recent years. They are not large in comparison with other areas of policy.

TABLE 12
Fiscal welfare : tax subsidies to owner-occupation, private pensions, life insurance and private health care (1982/3 £m)

	1978–9	1979–80	1980–1	1981–2	1982–3	1983–4
Owner-occupation:						
Mortgage interest relief	1820 (100%)	2050 (112%)	2320 (128%)	2150 (119%)	2500 (136%)	2620 (144%)
Capital gains tax exemption (f)	2500 (100%)	2800 (114%)	2850 (116%)	3000 (121%)	3000 (120%)	2400 (96%)
Stamp duty exemption	450 (100%)	325 (72%)	310 (68%)	300 (65%)	390 (85%)	415 (96%)
Exemption for tax on imputed income	'At least as large as mortgage interest relief'					
Pensions						
Tax exemption of contributions (e)	740 (100%)	700 (95%)	830 (112%)	1060 (145%)	1080 (147%)	1330 (180%)
Self-employed retirement Annuities	115 (100%)	155 (134%)	285 (247%)	330 (287%)	385 (334%)	430 (375%)
Life insurance						
Income tax exemption on premia (d)	425 (100%)	600 (142%)	640 (150%)	565 (133%)	580 (137%)	670 (160%)
Capital gains tax	75	155	140	140	180	150

Relief to employers on insurance contributions	No relief	25 (100%)	32 (120%)	40 (160%)	NA	NA

Notes:

(a) Many of the statistics are subject to a wide margin of error.

(b) The individual headings cannot be summed since the effect of each relief or allowance is costed separately.

(c) The private health care calculations are made by the author and are particularly uncertain.

(d) Abolished in 1984.

(e) Different methods of calculation produce figures varying from half to twice those quoted. See text for details.

(f) Reductions in the rate of capital gains tax in the last two years have affected the value of this exemption.

Sources: Public Expenditure White Papers from 1979 to 1984; Inland Revenue Statistics, 1983, p. 21; Provident Scheme Statistics, BUPA, PPP and WPA, 1983; *The Cost of Tax Relief for Pension Schemes*, Board of Inland Revenue, 1983.

Comparison of the figures with Table 9 indicates that the cost of the state of the expansion of private welfare is considerable. This has three implications. Firstly, in large measure privatisation is not a rolling back of the frontiers of the welfare state. It is rather the pursuit of state welfare programmes by other means. Fiscal subsidies, direct subventions (price cuts for council house sales, the assisted places scheme) and the framework of law (compulsory occupational sickness insurance) constrain and direct the rational choices people make just as much as compulsory taxation for state welfare does.

The second point concerns the argument developed earlier that privatisation policies have not led to sudden and radical changes in the shape of welfare. What they have done is build on long-run trends to enhance the social divisions implicit in state tolerance of public and private welfare. In this they complement the unemployment policy which has substantially worsened the position of the minority at the bottom of the income distribution, without damaging the mass of the working class.

The third point concerns this issue of privilege, of who gains most from tax subsidies to private welfare. The fact that real incomes rose on average by about 100 per cent between 1951 and 1981 and that disposable income after direct and indirect taxation increased at a rate only marginally slower meant that resources for the purchase of private services have been more widely available. The fiscal subsidies to owner-occupation and to pensions discussed earlier promoted the trend. The importance of private welfare in the maintenance of privilege may be illustrated in a number of ways. Mortgage interest relief was worth, on average, £125 a year to those whose income fell in the range under £3,000 in 1980/81; to those whose income exceeded £10,000 it was worth £520 (Pond, 1982, p. 67). Le Grand calculates that those in the top fifth of the income distribution receive some seven times as much as those in the bottom fifth in mortgage interest relief (Glennerster (ed.) 1983, p. 75). The success of top-ranking independent schools in gaining access for their pupils to the higher echelons of business, the judiciary, the civil services and armed forces and other privileged position in society is well-documented in the exhaustive research of the Newsom Committee (Maclure (ed.), 1973, pp. 336–8). Halsey et al. are able to demonstrate that attendance at either major independent or selective state sector schools made important differences to the opportunities of children throughout the period from the 1920s to the 1960s (1980, p. 171). As Abel-Smith points out 'it is still true that a child who attends wholly private education up to the age of eighteen can have more spent on him by the state than a child wholly in the state sector who gets no higher education' (Glennerster (ed.) 1983, p. 18). Little firm evidence of the social distribution of private medicine exists, although the Royal Commission on the NHS concluded that 'most individual subscriptions are taken out by . . . people with relatively high incomes' (Cmnd 7615, 1979, p. 289). The expansion of free medical insurance is charted by the Royal Commission on the Distribution of Income and Wealth from 26.4 per cent of managerial staff in 1973 to 44.1 per cent in 1978. In general such benefits go to the better-off: 'if account were taken of employee benefits . . . the dispersion of earnings would be increased' (Cmnd 7679, 1979, pp. 130 and 233). The expansion of occupational pensions is also likely to have benefited the better-off most. The redistribution of command over wealth that results from taking access to such schemes into account is 'confined to individuals . . . more than two-thirds of the way up the income distribution, as only about one-third of the population are members of occupational schemes' (Cmnd 7595, p. 107).

All these points indicate that the expansion of the private sector both enhances social divisions and is likely to confer real social advantages on its members. The fact that governments of neither party have seriously limited the opportunities for private-sector expansion and have maintained a structure of fiscal and other subsidies to it means that as the resources to pay for private welfare become available, growth follows.

Women's interests and welfare policy

The interests of feminists in recent developments in the welfare state have been focussed on two areas: the distinctive role of women in the wage-labour force as an industrial reserve army and their paradoxical role as dependants and as carers in the family. In the first area a number of writers have argued that women constitute a pool of labour readily available for wage-work (for example during the wars of the twentieth century or the industrial boom of the 1960s) but capable of being submerged as dependants of breadwinner husbands in the nuclear family when their work is not needed by industry. The advantage to capital is that the costs of maintaining women when not in paid work are borne through their husband's wages rather than through tax-financed social security, and that the availability of women dilutes the capacity of the core workforce to bid up wage rates when its work is in high demand (Beechey, 1977). The problem with this argument is that women are not spread evenly through the labour force, but concentrated in service industries, in non-manual work, in lower-paid work and in positions which lack authority (Reid and Wormald, 1982, ch. 6). This limits their capacity to serve as a reserve army of labour although it does indicate that they may provide an important section of the labour force in the current situation of decline in the manufacturing sector and expansion of the service sector. Breughel refines the reserve army of labour argument to suggest that *in a given sector of the economy*, individual women are more likely to lose jobs than comparable men in times of recession (1979). This contrasts with the more general claim that women as a group will be expelled from the labour force before men.

The extent to which the policies of recent governments have reinforced the distinctive position of women in the labour market is unclear. Cuts in state spending have had disproportionate effects on women's employment in welfare state services. For example, 50,000 women lost jobs due to the contraction of the school meals service between 1979 and 1983, and many more suffered substantial reductions in working hours and wages (Bull and Wilding, 1983, p. 48). The impact of the general rise in unemployment is less obvious (see Table 11). Female employment had grown by about 120,000 jobs a year up to 1980 although the male working population had been falling steadily, about 20,000 jobs a year being lost. The Department of Employment predicted that the increase would continue through the 1980s (April, 1981). However, the increase in women's employment ceased abruptly and by March 1983 the numbers of women in work had fallen from 9.5 million to about 8.6 million (Department of Employment, 1983, Table 1:1); a large number of women are likely to be excluded from official figures because they do not register for work. Estimates of the amount of concealed unemployment are vague. The most reliable source is a General Household survey question which showed that in 1981 some 6 per cent of unemployed men who wanted to work were not registered, as against 16 per cent of unmarried and 41 per cent of married women (OPCS, 1984, p. 81). The figures show a tendency for the numbers of unregistered unemployed to decline since the mid-1970s. On this basis the female unemployment rate should be increased by about 36 per cent (taking the balance of married and unmarried women under retirement age in the population into account). This indicates that women's unemployment may be much closer to male rates than official statistics indicate. If the estimate of the previous section that government policies account for at least half unemployment are applied to these figures, it appears that women's work opportunities have been substantially damaged by the government. This approach is likely to underestimate the importance of monetarism in relation to women's unemployment. Of the two factors which explain most of the increase in the unemployment rate which cannot be attributed to deficiencies in government policy, the most significant – the decline in the manufacturing sector – affects men more than women. Men continue to hold about three-quarters of the jobs in this sector as against three-fifths of all jobs.

The 1970 Equal Pay, 1975 Sex Discrimination and 1976 Employment Protection Acts may have had some effect in increasing the return to women workers. However, this should not be exaggerated. The modest improvement in the relative earnings of women workers gained by the Equal Pay legislation has suffered a reverse coinciding with the sharp increase in women's unemployment. The ratio of female to male average hourly earnings rose from 63 per cent in 1970 to 75 per cent in 1981. By 1982 it had fallen to under 74 per cent (CSO, 1984, p. 74).

The Sex Discrimination legislation has been widely criticised (see Oakley, 1982, p. 36; Coote and Campbell, 1982) as toothless. The Equal Opportunities Commission has failed to use the powers it has forcefully, launching six investigations and completing only one by 1980. The 1980 Employment Act weakens the rights to maternity pay and leave gained in 1976. In any case, research by Daniel (1980) shows that less than half of women employed during pregnancy actually obtained maternity pay under the stringent conditions of the 1976 Act.

In general, the policies of the 1979 government have damaged the position of women in work by diluting some of the moderate gains of the 1970s and through the impact of unemployment on women workers. Some advance in equal treatment under social security legislation has been made as a result of pressure from the European Community. From 1984 women are to have rights to claim sick and unemployment benefit increases for dependants comparable to those currently enjoyed by men and equal rights to family income supplement. Social security had followed Beveridge's assumption of household dependency enshrined in the dictum that a man's contributions are 'made on behalf of himself and his wife, as for a team' (1942, p. 49). The implied gender division of welfare is now only contained in the fact that some non-contributory benefits, available to comparatively small numbers of people, exclude housewives from entitlement. Of more importance is the failure of the system to give adequate recognition to women's work in the house. Currently the national insurance scheme only credits pension contributions at a minimal level to those who are not working due to domestic responsibilities. This means that women are unlikely to gain the same level of earnings-related pension as men with a continuous work record.

The assumed role of women as financial dependants reinforces the claim that they are available to provide unpaid care for groups in society which need it. Concern over this issue has intensified due to the community care policies which effectively throw the burden of responsibility for dependants on to families and on to women in families (Finch and Groves, 1980). However, the major burden of dependency has always been borne by women in families. Old age provides the most important example.

Between 1951 and 1981 the number of people over retirement age grew from 6.9 million to 9.9 million. This figure appears to have reached a plateau for the next two decades, although further problems for social policy are anticipated from the increases in the minority of frail 75 year olds within it (Cmnd 8789, vol. 2, p. 54, 1983). Only 2 per cent of those over 65 are cared for directly by the state in residential accommodation (Lewis, in Griffith (ed.), 1983, p. 119). This contrasts with the proportions cared for by children. In 1979–80 nearly 20 per cent of those over 85 were cared for by their children, and a further 10 per cent by children-in-law (Rimmer and Wicks in Glennerster (ed.), 1983, p. 32). In addition many have a considerable amount of contact with relatives. A survey conducted in 1976 showed that over half those over 65 received visits from relatives at least once a week, one-third several times a week (Hunt, 1978). The Study Commission on the Family concludes 'when it comes to day to day tasks . . . support from family members is more significant than that coming from the statutory social or health services' (1983, p. 29). Care is provided for the most part by middle-aged daughters, and state support services are structured around this assumption (Ungerson, 1982; Land and Parker, 1978). This tendency collides with the growing demands of labour force participation on married women. In 1951 just over 20 per cent of married women between 45 and 59 were in work. By 1966 the proportion had risen to 46 per cent and by 1979 to 61 per cent (General Household Survey, OPCS, 1980, Table 5.4). The rise in the numbers of women working accounted for almost all the two million increase in the working population between 1961 and 1975 (CSO, 1980). The expanding need for care collides with the shrinking reservoir of available carers. This is thrown into perspective by Eversley's calculation that the typical couple married in 1920 and alive in the early 1980s would have some 42 female relatives of whom a third would not be in paid employment. In contrast the typical couple married in 1950 are likely to have only 11 living female relatives of whom only three will not have paid jobs by the time the couple reach their eightieth birthday (cited in Hadley and Hatch, 1981, p. 90). The problem results not from new welfare policies, but from the continuing unwillingness of the state to take more than a small part of this burden from families. The impact on women is due to the way in which the ideology of the family thrusts them into the role of dependants who are thus available to care.

The other important development in patterns of family life is the increase in the numbers of female-headed families, since the early 1960s, from about a quarter of a million in 1961 to about a million in 1981. Roughly one-third of these are dependent on supplementary benefit. The failure to provide an adequate system of benefits for this group is an indication of the failure of the welfare state to acknowledge the needs of those with responsibility for children outside marriage. This failure reaches back to the refusal of the post-war government to enact Beveridge's proposals for separation benefits and adequate child allowances.

Recent policies have clearly affected the interests of women in the spheres of work and the family. The most important changes have been the failure to tackle unemployment effectively, and the failure to develop policies to cope with changes in the availability of family care and in patterns of family life. In a nutshell, the problem is monetarism plus the inertia of the welfare state rather than new departures in social policy.

Conclusion

The review of current changes in policy in this chapter suggests that in general it is not so much specific changes in the constitution and organisation of the welfare state that are important in altering the impact of welfare as factors outside the welfare state. In the case of cuts and restructuring the most important issue is the pursuit of a monetarist economic policy which produces higher levels of unemployment than would otherwise exist. The only area of substantial cuts is council house spending. The plans for privatisation of welfare have not been realised. The continued effect of concessions, subsidies and fiscal reliefs has caused the private sector to pursue an existing trend to expansion. The scope for future expansion may be limited. The implications of current policy for women concern two areas: on the one hand the effect of unemployment on women's job opportunities and the failure of government to make equal pay legislation any more effective. On the other the impact of changes in patterns of work and family formation on community care policies. The importance of changes, in any case, lies in their effect on minorities: unemployment penalises the out-of-work; such growth as takes place in the private sector directs privilege to upper income groups. Minorities of women are affected by demands for the care of dependants. For the majority the welfare state is pursuing business very much as usual. The pattern of encouragement for privatisation, for a family ethic and of suspicion of welfare spending is in any case a long-term phenomenon, rather than a fresh departure of the late 1970s.

Just as the welfare state did not follow a pleasant path through the gardens of consensus to the precipice of crisis, so the extent to which current changes cut across the even tenor of past policy should not be exaggerated. In the next chapter we move on to consider why the new crisis theory is popular, if alternative explanations of events are possible.

5
Ideology and continuity

The tradition of all the dead generations weighs like a nightmare
on the brain of the living.
> Karl Marx, *The Eighteenth Brumaire
> of Louis Bonaparte.*

Let us say we are trying to understand the goals and values of a
certain group, or grasp their vision of the polity; we might try to
probe this by a questionnaire asking them whether they assent
or not to a number of propositions, which are meant to express
different goals, evaluations, beliefs. But how did we design the
questionnaire? How did we pick these propositions? Here we
relied on our understanding of the goals, values, visions
involved. But then this our understanding can be challenged,
and hence the significance of our results questioned. Perhaps
the finding of our study, the compiling of proportions of assent
and dissent to these propositions is irrelevant, is without
significance for understanding the agents or the polity concerned.
> Charles Taylor, *Interpretation
> and the Science of Man*

So far this book has attempted to draw together evidence from a
range of sources relevant to three different areas of welfare state
studies: public opinion about social welfare; the development of
the welfare state; and recent welfare politics. A number of writers
have suggested that the 1970s and 1980s have been characterised

by sea-change, crisis or abrupt departures in all three areas. The argument of preceding chapters claims that the reality is rather less exciting. Public attitudes to welfare show strong support for the major state services, coupled with much weaker enthusiasm for the less favoured services for minority groups. There is an equally strong support for the private sector, with a consequent ambivalence between state and market. The family ethic is rather less marked. Attitudes to state welfare are influenced by many factors, the strongest of which seem to be judgments of self-interest.

The story of the welfare state since the Second World War does not bear out the pattern of a shift from welfare consensus to conflict that some writers describe: nor does it mark the decline from a golden age of Beveridge and universalism. Social policy appears to have always been a topic for political debate. The structure of the welfare state has shown an equal concern to divide favoured from unfavoured services, to allow a well-guarded space for the nurturing of private provision and to categorise women in families as dependants and care-givers at the same time, throughout its history. If these features catch the eye more in the recent past it is because various changes have taken place in the context of the welfare state – economic constraint, a general rise in affluence, the incursion of monetarism, and a transformation of the pattern of family life. These make perennial issues more prominent. They do not generate new departures in policy or ideology.

The outcome of all these arguments is to focus attention on the power of inertia in social policy. The overall theme is of the persistence of certain themes, topics and tendencies, of continuity rather than crisis, of business as usual, given the inevitable changes. The central question becomes why should this be so? The question is the more pressing since current welfare policies seem less appropriate to the realities of family organisation, employment and economic policy than they can ever have been.

Many factors contribute to an explanation of the development of the welfare state and of ideas about it since the Second World War. In different ways Titmuss (1976, p. 82), Thane (1982, pp. 263–7) and Gough (1979, ch. 5) point to the significance of the social, economic and political changes of total war and the exceptional period of sustained growth which followed it. Other writers point to specific British institutional characteristics – the apparatus of accommodation between government, unions and business interests that generated a corporatist and stabilising approach to policy (Middlemas, 1979), the peculiar national sentiment that is the heritage of imperial grandeur (Hall et al., 1978), the defensive strength of the trade union movement coupled with the lack of a mass socialist political party (Westergaard and Resler, 1975, part 5). Within the welfare state other interests operate – pension funds (Kincaid, 1975, ch. 8), building societies (Ginsburg, 1979, p. 131), the professional groupings of doctors (Forsyth, 1966), and teachers (Locke, 1974, p. 27). The nature of the expansion of state-sector employment and the extension of unionisation and industrial militancy within it (Gough, 1979, p. 142) pose further limits to state action. The changes in class structure and loosening bond between class and party provide an additional arena for manoeuvre in policy to gain political support (see, for example, Butler and Kavanagh, 1979; Coates, 1980). The increasing salience of taxation may constrain the development of welfare programmes (Klein, 1980, p. 25).

All these factors, in interaction with many others, can be woven into the story. The approach here is different. The emphasis is on the overall pattern of consistency and the broad-brush portrait of the factors that underlie rather than the micro-politics of day-to-day struggle. The underlying assumption is that in general in the long-run people's political aspirations and support are the outcome of their ideas. Even in the case of pressure for self-interest, a conception of what that interest is must direct the demand. Chapters 2, 3 and 4 suggest that the ambivalences in public opinion about welfare are more or less reflected in the overall tendencies of policy.

We focus on the contribution that accounts of dominant currents in ideas can make to understanding the development of welfare. The answer is given in terms of the influence of social life in an advanced capitalist society which organises family life on a patriarchal basis, on every-day common sense thinking – in terms of the organisation of ideology. This involves on the one hand the claim that the roots of ideology can be found in particular features of social life and on the other the argument that patterns of ideology are major influences on social policy, on mass opinion and on the development of social science. Both claims are contested. However, the advantage of an approach through ideology is that it offers the possibility of linking together the three areas of discourse covered in this book in a way in which no other approach does. Moreover, if the appeal is to relatively stable foundations for ideology, the consistency of ideas and policy is explained.

Ideology

The notion of ideology involves the claim that people's ideas, beliefs, attitudes and values are not simply to be taken for granted, but that they admit of explanation: that coherent accounts of the consistencies and changes in ideas can be given. Since patterns in ideas about society play a major part in making society possible (although opinion varies on how large that part is) this is a large and fundamental claim. Discussion of ideology is multi-faceted and diffuse. We shall attempt a brief review of the use of the concept with special reference to the state. The review will attempt to set out the main approaches, the problem they encounter and the usefulness of the idea in relation to the theme of the book.

The development of the notion

The concept of ideology in social science is directly analogous to that of irony in drama. Both rest on the claim that there is an opposition between appearance and reality in the meanings that can be given to a situation (Muecke, 1972, p. 7). Just as the resolution of dramatic irony depends on the supplanting of confusion or distortion by the truth, so the idea that consciousness is mystified implies the possibility of a correct knowledge of social relations.

Most work traces the prehistory of the notion of ideology to various intellectual strands in the break-up of the medieval world order and its supersession by the modern era (Larrain, 1979, ch. 1). The critical currents generated by the liberation struggles of the bourgeoisie provoked a new analysis of the forces that made society stable and led people to accept particular forms of government. Three strands in the turmoil may be picked out: a critique of traditional politics, a critique of traditional science and a critique of traditional religion.

Machiavelli's insights into the political practice of rulers included a distinction between fraud and force as the bases of power. While it is virtually impossible to acquire dominion 'simply by the use of open and undisguised force' this 'can quite well be done by using only fraud' (Machiavelli, 1970, p. 311). Political power may be rooted in conspiracy. Hobbes united the critique of politics with the scientific critique of religion. Here he built on Bacon's methodological work. Bacon is concerned to distinguish empirical reality from distortion in the sphere of knowledge of the natural world as Machiavelli does in the political arena. Thus various 'idols' derived from habit, the passions, language and traditional theories are identified which stand as obstacles to the progress of knowledge based on observation. Hobbes takes the empiricist method to its logical conclusion to point out that there are many things that knowledge based on experience cannot explain. This is the root of religion: 'ignorance of natural causes disposes a man to credulity' (Hobbes, 1968, p. 169).

At the same time the individualist premise that people act only out of self-interest leads to the view that they have 'a perpetual and restless desire of power after power, that ceaseth only in death' (Hobbes, 1968, ch. 13). This is because the work of others can benefit the power-holder. The problem is to explain how political order is possible given that the 'natural condition of mankind' is a 'war of each against all'. The solution is the assumption that social order is founded on a covenant, a contract for mutual benefit, which combines prudential with moral obligation: any order is better than chaos; because the primal contract may be referred to, all subjects are morally bound to obey the sovereign (Raphael, 1970, p. 88). The desirability of political order justifies the sovereign in using any technique, including the promoting of religion in order to reinforce authority. The prudential argument is closely paralleled by modern socio-biology (Rose and Rose, 1982; Sayers, 1982, pp. 60–1). Hobbes has linked science, politics and religion. The scientific critique of religion shows how religious fiction can contribute to political order and this can serve a common interest. The distinction between surface appearance and reality is evident in each area.

A direct emphasis on the role of ideas as a positive force in society emerges with the French Enlightenment. De Tracy is the first author to use the term 'ideology'. In his work it refers to a 'natural history of ideas' which is concerned to trace ideas to their origins in sensation and thereby enable the production of a critique of current theories and of a true and universal theory of human nature. The *philosophes* of this tradition hoped to produce the educational programme for the new society of post-revolutionary France. As Hall points out (1977, p. 10), their interaction with the political order is instructive: 'Napoleon took them up in 1799, in the "moment" of Brumaire, in order to win support in . . . the educated middle class . . . but by 1803, the "moment" of his Concordat with the Church, he abandoned them, deliberately setting out to destroy the Institute's core.' He was the first to use 'ideologist' in a derogatory sense, to mean unrealistic and arrogant intellectual.

Comte, one of the founders of positivism, developed a critique of theological and metaphysical thought which pointed to science as the road to knowledge shorn of ideological presupposition. This approach supports political conclusions: 'all social mechanisms rest upon opinions' (quoted in Larrain, 1979, p. 29). The upshot is a Wellsian vision of a future in which scientifically based government will usher in a rational order. This conception has been widely criticised because it reintroduces metaphysics in its linking of science and social progress at the same time as ideology is banished in conjunction with an unscientific world order (Durkheim, 1964, pp. 18–20; Huxley, quoted in Larrain, 1979, p. 30; Gould, 1969, p. 41; Plamenatz, 1963).

German idealism developed the critique of religion and its relation to politics in a different direction. Hegel drew an opposition between the dogmatic form in which Christianity developed historically and the true object of religion which is centred on the infinite and is the same as the object of philosophy. Social institutions alienate mankind from its true concern, introducing a mystification of reality. The school that followed Hegel developed explanations of this paradox. The most important was Feuerbach who directly influenced Marx.

Feuerbach's contribution was to solve the problem by reversing its terms. God becomes the projection of the human essence. 'Man – this is the mystery of religion – projects his being into objectivity and then again makes himself an object to this projected image of himself thus converted into a subject . . .' (1957, p. 29). The oppression of human thought by organised religion is not the result of the self-interested activity of a priestly caste: it is self-created by the human race. It does not result from simple weakness or credulity as Hobbes suggested. The divine essense is real, it is to be found within humanity. The argument is parallel to Blake's fable of how men imbued nature with divinity and finally forgot that 'all deities reside in the human breast' (1927, p. 47). The opposition to reality is a distinction that is self-generated. Appearance is the central concept developed by Marx in the spheres of knowledge and politics. To do this Marx developed a historical account of the production and projection of ideas that went beyond the simple assumption of free-floating, universal religious sentiment.

The main theme in the prehistory of ideology has been the distinction between appearances and reality in human affairs; in politics, where conspiracy is seen as essential to order by Machiavelli and Hobbes; in science, where a method to delve behind the illusion of appearances was sought by Bacon and

Comte; and in religion where an explanation of the dominion of traditional ideas against progressive ideals was sought by Comte and Feuerbach. The development of ideas runs from the simple exposition of illusion as conspiracy – as fraud in Machiavelli or priestly deceit in the pre-Feuerbachian critics of religion – to the projection of human reality and its apprehension in a distorted form by Feuerbach.

Marx: ideology as a social product

Marx's work on ideology contains three elements which are of enormous importance: the source of ideas in social action, the production of distorted images of society through social conflict, and the existence of ambivalent or self-contradictory patterns of ideas.

The central text in Marx's work which describes his methodological presuppositions is well known:

> In the social production which men carry on they enter into definite relations which are indispensable and independent of their will; these relations of production correspond to a definite stage of development of their material powers of production. The sum total of these relations of production constitutes the economic structure of society – the real foundation, on which rise legal and political superstructures and to which correspond definite forms of social consciousness. The mode of production in material life determines the general character of the social, political and spiritual processes of life. It is not the consciousness of men that determines their existence, but, on the contrary, their social existence determines their consciousness (1959, p. 84).

The basis of society is economic production; production is a social activity and leads to the production of goods to meet needs and of ideas and institutions. This approach leads immediately to a historical development of Feuerbach's account of ideology. The process whereby the human essence is projected and distorted rests on the nature of production in different historical periods. These may be characterised by the material forces of production available and the social relations of production. It is the latter area that is important to any analysis of ideology that is not to rest on mere technology.

Why focus on production? Why make this social process the starting point for theory rather than resting analysis on political relations or on the currents in ideas that are dominant at particular times? Marx's answer is simple: without production to satisfy needs there won't be any society, and this is a matter of brute fact, not logic:

> Men can be distinguished from animals by consciousness, by religion or anything else you like. They themselves begin to produce their means of subsistence, a step which is conditioned by their physical organisation . . . The way in which men produce their means of subsistence depends first of all on the nature of the actual means of subsistence they find in existence and have to reproduce . . . The nature of individuals . . . depends on the material conditions determining their production (Marx and Engels, 1970, p. 42).

This does not mean that the description of arrangements to satisfy brute need is an adequate account of society. The situation of humanity in a natural world necessitates action to meet needs. The process is a 'double relationship'. On the one hand the social co-operation is conditioned by natural needs. On the other the form of that co-operation continually produces fresh needs.

If human action is rendered essential by the constitution of the natural world, it is not a simple reflex that can be explained in terms of the action of that world. Thus Marx escapes on the one hand the dualist tradition that originated in Descartes and which traced the separate realities of consciousness and nature, ultimately finding the problem of how real contact with nature could be possibly insoluble. On the other hand he avoids the perspective of British empiricism through Hobbes, Locke and Hume that influenced the French *philosophes* in the work of De Tracy and resulted in the claim that all knowledge was based on contact with the external world through the senses. From both perspectives a fundamental distinction between appearance and reality which condemns ideology to the status of mere illusion incapable of correction by knowledge seems inevitable. In the former rationalist tradition, the gulf occurs with Kant's reality of noumenal objects, theoretically necessary in order to guarantee the consistency of the phenomenal reality which knowing subjects experience, but impossible for them to contact directly. In the latter empiricism, the impossibility of providing a rational basis for the categories used to organise sense-data into knowledge leads to a similar despair in the hope of correction of ideology: the *philosophes* lapse into a fragile idealism.

The notion of action used by Marx to link nature to consciousness is not simply conditioned by nature but contains elements of human purpose:

> What distinguishes the worst architect from the best of bees is this, that the architect raises his structure in imagination before he erects it in reality. At the end of every labour-process we get a result that already existed in the imagination of the labourer at its commencement (1974, p. 174).

Yet labour is not simply the transformation of nature: it is also the transformation of people's relations with each other. The ways in which labour can be carried out affect the social relations of production. On the most general scale:

> People make their own history, but they do not make it just as they please: they do not make it under circumstances chosen by themselves, but under circumstances directly encountered, given and transmitted from the past (Marx and Engels, 1970, p. 360).

The link between appearance and reality is a double process: survival requires human action on a natural world; human consciousness makes that action purposive and collective; people project a plan upon the world which is given back to them in their technical and social creations; finally these creations form the circumstances under which history continues. Ideology is a human product conditioned by the human development of society against a natural world.

Ideology and capitalism

In all class societies the labour of workers produces a surplus which is extracted by a non-working class. Marx regarded his account of the process whereby exploitation took place in 'the very Eden of Liberty, Equality and Bentham' as the most important discovery in his account of capitalism. It is the basis of his theory of ideology.

The problem is to explain how a market system, which functions through the exchange of equivalents (at least by and large, in the long run) can allow systematic exploitation. The answer is that exploitation is built into the basic institution of the market – alienable private property. Marx argued that the value of goods was related to the amount of work required to produce them. The same applies to the workers' capacity to work. Thus pay fluctuates about the average cost of the goods that a given worker consumes. However, human labour has the unique property that it can produce more than its value: correctly used people can produce goods worth more than the equivalent of the value of their own labour-time. The capitalist extracts a profit, while paying the worker the market worth of the labour used. The point is that society is divided by the institution of private property into two classes: those who own and control the capital goods which enable them to pump out profits from the employment of those who have nothing to sell but their ability to work. Two classes with contradictory interests confront each other. The central problem of this approach is the issue of how stability is possible. The core of an answer to this question operates at the level of ideas, and is summed up in the notion of 'commodity fetishism'. This explains how people's interests in capitalist society, which are at heart class interests, are experienced as individual: people confront each other as buyers and sellers of commodities, seeking to maximise their own command. They may of course form alliances, interest groups, unions, cartels with this individual interest in mind. The fact that it is because capitalists as a social force own and have control over the means of production, and that workers have no real choice in working for capital that capital is able to extract profits slips out of focus. Because the goods that people make and need become private property in the market, interests are apprehended as individual and not collective. This underlies the way groups and classes struggle for their interests as they see them. It explains why capitalism has enormous reserves of resilience in such conflict.

Human action in class society produces a distorted understanding of that society, because the natural conditions which can satisfy needs are understood as private property. The relationship between appearance and reality becomes inverted: people's collective work, projected on to the world, returns as profit, capital goods and commodities, as things rather than social relations. This perpetuates the oppressions of class society.

Parallel to this process, the existence of a separate state which is a centre of formal power and does not enter into the market as an individual commodity actor, generates its own set of ideological associations. The political sphere is formally separated from the economic. If the system is understood to be more or less democratic, the state can be seen as standing against the market. In contrast to the market where the impersonal operations of law of supply and demand allocate resources, the government is capable of making decisions based on discussion, negotiation, reconciliation. It can arbitrate between the different antagonistic interests of the market and produce an agreed and normatively justified solution. Again human political actions are distorted: the oppression of the private property system is experienced simply as an individual relation in the market. Collective political relations are projected into a separate sphere where a basic ground-rule is the protection of the private property system itself.

The central theme in these accounts of ideology is of a dissolution of the concept of a division between appearance and reality that had underlain previous accounts of ideology. Marx is claiming that in one sense the experience of capitalist society is misleading, alienated, mystified or confused. Yet it is clear that if this had been the sum total of his critique he would simply have produced moral condemnations of its wrongness or have regarded it as sufficient to expose incorrect apprehensions. He does neither (Wood, 1972, p. 245; Geras, 1972, p. 305). The distorted communication is a particular reality generated by human action under particular circumstances. It is the reflection of a particular projection of the human essence of labour. The claim to alienation results from the fact that this reflection obscures a larger view. In the market interests are individual – the supersession of the market can only result from the apprehension of interests as collective. In capitalism, the legitimate role of the state is to maintain the market. This implies that no wider view of social development is possible. Marx's central concern was to look beyond the blinkers, to envisage a society wherein a collective perspective was available on the surface.

How has Marx's contribution to ideology structured subsequent thought? It is convenient to organise work between the poles provided by the twin theoretical dilemmas of marxist analysis.

New developments in ideology

Marx's original statement that roots ideas in social existence understood as productive activity is immediately vulnerable to attack from two directions. As Plamenatz (1975, p. 282) and Russell (1961, p. 751) point out, if the notion that social existence determines consciousness is interpreted in a rigid and individual-istic sense, the theory immediately collapses. To claim that the direction of every individual person's thought is laid down on tramlines by society is to move to the view that there is no alternative, that there is therefore no truth or falsehood. All thought is as it is and all social theory (including Marx's theory of ideology) merits no discussion. The discussion would be pre-determined by social existence and could not advance to a more correct view. The link between ideas and mode of production must be interpreted as looser than this, to claim that particular modes of production tend to foster the general acceptance of particular climates of ideas.

The problem now is that the approach wobbles too far the other way. If ideas are dependent on mode of production and modes of production change, then the basis of ideas changes and theory is plunged immediately into relativism. The solution to this problem contained in Marx rests on the orderliness and rigidity of modes of production. The development of history is unidirectional and has a goal. Indeed it is this aspect of marxist thought that leads Hobsbawm to regard it as superior to other modes of historio-graphy, because it has a criterion to make sense of human affairs (1972, p. 282). The goal is communist society and the values and theories generated in other social forms can be judged by the yard-stick of that form of social relations.

The subsequent development of marxist work on ideology can be traced as a track between the precipices of relativism and determinism, the former derived from an overstatement of the power of the world of appearance, the latter from that of material reality. The problem is to link them adequately.

The determinist traditional rested most heavily on the inter-pretation of Engels by Plekhanov and Lenin and is most strongly represented in the current German School. The relativist tradition may be traced through those influenced by the sociology of knowledge and of literature, through Goldmann, and structural-ism, although the work of Lukács and Gramsci on class-conscious-ness has been of substantial importance. The injection of a Freudian psychoanalysis of ideology by the Frankfurt School is of importance, as is the development of ideology by non-marxist writers such as Mannheim and Berger and Luckmann. More recently attempts have been made to bridge both traditions in the work of Althusser in France and of Stuart Hall and his associates in the UK.

Engels developed the conception of the ideological sphere and indeed the whole superstructure of society as having an indepen-dent existence, which is ultimately subsidiary to that of the economic base. This idea we shall see re-emerging in the work of Althusser. In a letter to Schmidt he writes: 'although the material mode of existence is the *primum agens* this does not prevent the ideological spheres from reacting against it and influencing it in their turn, but this is a secondary effect' (quoted in Larrain, 1979, p. 70).

Elsewhere the role of the material base is more simply dominant and consciousness becomes an 'image', a 'reflection', a 'conscious reflex of the dialectical notion of the real world' (Engels, 1970, p. 609). Labriola and Plekhanov develop a theory of mediations between the economic structure, which is the ultimate determining factor, and the directly and indirectly moulded world of ideas. The trajectory of this attempt to spell out the nature of economic determination is much simplified in the work of Lenin. For him, Marx's decisive contribution to science is the proof of the historical necessity of socialism by an objective analysis of capitalism and its place in history. Lenin's work leads him to play down the role of ideology in social order. The power of the state becomes (in an exposition of Engels's *Origin of the Family, Private Property and the State*) simply the power of 'special bodies of armed men which have prisons etc. at their command' (1965, p. 10). The upshot is that issues of legitimacy and allegiance do not figure in the account. The central problem is the physical 'smashing' of the bourgeois state. Callinicos argues that it is the triumph of this approach in the debates of the Third International and its expression in the vulgar evolutionism of Stalin's *Dialectical and Historical Materialism* that went hand in hand with a politics of blood (1976, p. 23). If people's ideas are more or less determined by their class location, there is little point in trying to change their minds by argument.

The development of determinism in recent years is most apparent in the work of recent German writers popularised by Holloway and Picciotto (1978). Here the notion of the state is more sophisticated and attempts to come to terms with the massive expansion in economic intervention of this century. However, the account of the pattern of ideas is ultimately equally determinist.

The central problem tackled in this work is that of the *form* of the capitalist state: why does a state power exist in capitalist societies that is understood by citizens to be separate from the economic relations of the market? A simple answer is implicit in the work of Altvater: there are functions that must be assumed by the state 'due to the impossibility of their being performed by individual capitals' (p. 42). This is essentially parallel to Friedman's analysis of a role for the state where the market will not provide since the product will give other users a free ride: here the scope is expanded to include infrastructure and social control. The approach is clearly functionalist and the extension of necessary state activities to include the production of legitimating ideology (cf. Blanke, Jurgens and Kastendiek, 1978, p. 109) does not resolve this. Other writers, most importantly Hirsch, graft on an historical account of the derivation of the state form that rests on the argument that a society where needs are met through private property produces an individualisation of interests: this leads to the demand that the state defend the system of private interests as a whole. The editors of the volume are concerned to point out the limitation of this approach: 'it is not that form analysis represents some "royal road to science" . . . if the reader finds the debate at times too formal and too abstract, this criticism is partly justified' (1978, p. 30). They appeal for the injection of a focus on class struggle into the analysis in order to provide an historically dynamic component. However, this has not so far been achieved. The result is that form analysis produces a determinism resting on an account of the ideas about the state appropriate to an abstract notion of capitalist relations.

The relativist tradition, on the other hand, divorces ideas so absolutely from society that a number of representations of appearance may carry equal weight and the end result is an impossibility of linking any of them to an assertion about reality. This problem has dogged the sociology of knowledge tradition. Mannheim was concerned to tackle ideas at the most general level: 'the crucial question is how the totality we call the spiritual "Weltanschauung" of an epoch can be distilled from the various "objectivications" of that epoch – and how we can given an account of it' (1968, p. 73). The problem of making sense of different world views lies in finding a way of grounding particular interpretations of them.

Mannheim tackles this issue through a distinction between partial and total concepts of ideology. The first notion refers to a scepticism towards certain propositions of an adversary, the second to an attempt to understand their entire system of thought. This finds its natural home in a relational understanding. The problem of moving to a total analysis of a world view, yet retaining some epistemological foundation which enables one to ground an interpretation of that world view, remains.

The most important recent expression of this dilemma is found in the work of Berger and Luckmann. For them, the sociology of knowledge operates as an idealist dialectic:

> Society is a human product, Society is an objective reality, Man is a social product: . . . any analysis of the social world that leaves out one of these three moments will be distortive (1966, p. 79).

The problem is to give an account of the consistencies and regularities in the production of society if it is simply understood as human product, in which nature has no part. This leads the writers to place considerable emphasis on an empirically grounded account of internalisation and socialisation, which occupies about half the book. If it is this kind of social process that is to provide a foundation for social knowledge, it is hard to see how the approach is to avoid the kind of determinism for which Talcott Parsons's structural functionalism was criticised.

Within marxism a relativist tendency is evident in those who attempt to compensate economic determinism by postulating an independent role for consciousness. Perhaps the most important influence in recent years was Gramsci who builds on Lukács's early writings. In his early work Lukács was concerned to emphasise the role of consciousness in revolution: marxism is the ideology of the proletariat because it explains and promotes revolution. Legality on the other hand is the major ideological obstacle to proletarian consciousness because it involves respect for the status quo. Ideology is set at the centre of the stage in the explanation of social stability. 'The strength of every society is in the last resort a spiritual strength' (1971, p. 262). Gramsci traces out the role of ideology in history in more detail.

His starting point is the conception of class hegemony – the ability of one class to establish a moral and intellectual leadership over other classes, without resort to the use of force. The political implication is that it is possible for the working class to establish a proletarian hegemony in civil society and through this means achieve control of the state and of the future direction of society. Anderson criticises this approach for its emphasis on ideology as a creature of civil society and its separation of the ideological hegemony of the bourgeoisie and state power. To the contrary, so long as the authority of legitimate democratic forms is maintained, the bourgeoise state is 'the principal ideological lynchpin of Western Capitalism' (1977, p. 28). The role of ideology conceived as an autonomous force of consciousness in social change is overplayed. Ideology tends to float free from material relations.

Two further developments have complicated the analysis of ideology. Firstly Freudian psychoanalysis posits a different distinction between appearance and reality in the conscious and the unconscious. A range of writers loosely centred about the Frankfurt School have attempted to incorporate this into sociological work. Secondly the distinction between linguistic structure and the meanings constructed in given communications developed by Sassure and Frege and the Prague Circle offers a second

107

opposition utilised by Goldmann and by recent French Structuralist thought.

The central concept of the Frankfurt School is of an alienation of humanity from an inner reality by social processes. In the work of Fromm the idea is of 'estrangement from the world' . . . a person's 'acts and their consequences have become his masters' (1963, p. 120). Marcuse argues that capitalism requires a surplus repression of instinctive drives in order to maintain an unhealthy compulsion toward accumulation and acquisitiveness (1956, p. 37).

Goldmann develops an analysis of all social processes as significative structures which can only be understood in terms of their genesis (1970). Interpretation requires a wider analysis – at the widest level, a world view. Which world view is to be preferred? 'That which offers the widest form and range of comprehension' (1973, p. 53). The problem of course is how criteria for range and width are themselves to be grounded. The approach is forever vulnerable to erosion by infinite regress.

The development of theory about ideology, conceived as a gulf between appearance and reality, has led to a disproportionate emphasis on one side or the other with the result that bridges fail to reach across. Three recent writers have developed eclectic approaches designed to span the gulf.

The work of Althusser draw both on Engels's conception of science and on recent semiology. It has been mainly responsible for restoring the concept of ideology to the forefront of debate. It is widely criticised (Therborn, 1980; Hirst, 1976; Callinicos, 1976; Larrain, 1979) so it is worth pointing out its importance.

Althusser offers a theory that attempts to link science and practice, the experience of subjectivity and the marxist account of objective historical processes, and the aspects of the state as legitimate ideological power and bearer of physical force. He thus tackles problems that many of his detractors do not acknowledge.

The Structuralist approach is pursued in an account of ideology as itself bridging appearance and reality: 'In ideology men do indeed express, not the relation between them and their conditions of existence, but the way they live the relation between them and their conditions of existence. This pre-supposes both a real relation and an "imaginary" "lived" relation' (1977, p. 233). Thus the problem of the extremes of determinism and relativism is solved by taking both on board. Both strands are developed. Can they be reconciled?

Ideology is envisaged as a necessary social cement, essential to all social order, even that of communist society. In this sense ideology as a category 'is eternal exactly like the unconscious' (1972, p. 152) or, one might add, Sassure's linguistic structure. Particular ideologies exist according to the circumstances of particular situations. The subordinated class can only generate an ideology which leads to social change through science, an approach that parallels that of Lenin.

The central epistemological role of ideology is to 'interpellate', to address and construct individuals as subjects in a reality that is actually produced by the relations of social classes. The experience of subjectivity, of self as social actor, results from the timeless social category of ideology. Thus the view of history as class struggle is reconciled with the experience of individual autonomy.

Althusser links appearance and reality by positing ideology on both sides of the gulf. Reality is always and inevitably experienced as appearance which always and inevitably stands in a necessary relation to reality. The experience of subjectivity, which makes the illusion of relativism possible, is part of the process of generation of appearance. The inevitability of ideology renders the system determinist: the place in it for human action is unclear. At the same time, the importation of inevitable subjectivity introduces an inescapable relativism in the realm of ideas. The problem of distinguishing scientific thought from ideology becomes insuperable. Ultimately Althusser claims there can be no touchstone for correct knowledge. The relation of theory and practice is obscured by the divorce of theory from the real world as 'the theory of theoretical practice'. Debray comments that thus 'all we have to do to become good theoreticians is to be lazy bastards!' (1973, p. 187). Althusser's approach fails to find a satisfactory reconciliation of materialism and ideas. The link through ideology becomes ineluctable and determinist.

The second approach is that of Habermas. He offers an influential approach to the problems of legitimacy of the modern state (see Offe, 1974, p. 54; Dunleavy, 1980, p. 43; Gough, 1979). The emphasis on psychoanalysis as the tool for exploration of inner space in earlier work enables him to distinguish a separate sphere of motives in addition to the traditional division between politics and economics in marxist analysis of capitalist society. In laissez-faire capitalism, the legitimate role of the state was to service the system of private property through pursuit of a minimal role. This system provided the sphere of pursuit of goals and offered the potential of legitimation because it was experienced as operating through the agency of impersonal market forces. The dilemma that arises as the state is forced (by crisis trends and class struggle) to intervene more and more in the market is that the pattern of interventions may tend to contradict the market interests of particular groups. There is no way that legitimacy can be guaranteed. However, this theory is more than the theory of the collision of a 'common interest' state with particular market interests as it intervenes in the market. This is the approach of state overload theorists in Anglo-Saxon political science (Beer, 1982; Rose, 1980). Habermas's central point is that the legitimation crisis is 'at root a crisis of motivation' (1976, p. 380). It is the cultural sphere that provides motives and it is unable to provide a pattern of motives appropriate to the suppression of some private property interests and the advance of others in the stabilisation of advanced market society. The clash is between ideology as a pattern of motives and the political necessities of capitalism.

It is unclear whether this theory offers a determinism or not. The incapacity of the state to produce the motives it needs to ensure allegiance is asserted. Yet crisis-trends are mere 'theorems' requiring further empirical investigation. In this sense, it is uncertain whether the individualist rigours of psychoanalysis are adequately married to the possibilities of history.

The third writer is Stuart Hall, who with a number of associates has produced an influential series of papers and books. These place a central role on the analysis of communication in the production of ideology. The central idea is summed up in a paper on television discourse (1973). This rests on the semiology of Barthes which points to the gap between linguistic structure and the social circumstances that construct its interpretation and give it meaning. Hall, however, is able to develop this in two important directions: he takes on board the Gramscian tradition with its analysis of class cultural hegemony; and he refers back to an older tradition of Marxist theory with its fundamental emphasis on the material determinants of ideology.

The most important factor in the social context of communication is (following Gramsci) the 'hegemonic viewpoint'. This:

(a) defines within its terms the mental horizon, the universe of possible meanings of a whole society or culture; and
(b) carries within it the stamp of legitimacy – it appears coterminous with what is 'natural', 'inevitable' taken for granted about the social order (p. 17).

Since broadcasters are part of the social order, it is not surprising that their professional codes reflect the hegemonic order. Thus the ideology of a dominant class sets the context for the transmission of information. However, everyday-life experience also contributes to understanding: it determines the plausibility of different media messages. Hegemony can only be maintained so long as it makes sense in terms of the recipient of information's common-sense world view. This analysis of the way cultural context produces ideology has proved especially fruitful in the work of the Glasgow University Media Group (1976) and of the Birmingham Centre for Contemporary Cultural Studies. So far, the school associated with Hall has produced a series of brilliant but unrelated insights into specific cultural contexts. These 'set-pieces' include a prescient account of the appeal of the ideology of the new right to ordinary people (Hall, 1979); an analysis of how it comes about that rough working-class teenagers are prepared to accept a second-rate schooling that leads to the poorest life-chances (Willis, 1978); and a series of essays on the development of racism in the UK in recent years and of the state policies which nourish it (Birmingham Centre, 1982). The problem that confronts this approach is how these separate penetrations of hegemonic ideology are to be welded into a general account of the experience of everyday life which explains the plausibility of ideas and assumptions which benefit the ruling class.

The three approaches to the problem of generating a marxist theory of ideology that does not overbalance in the direction of relativism on the one hand, or determinism on the other are not successful. In Althusser's approach ideology becomes a reflex of history, in Habermas's the relation between ideas and social circumstances is ultimately unclear and Hall does not give a final answer to the question. However, there do appear to be consistent patterns in ideas about the welfare state, and this fact justifies an attempt to theorise them. Here we attempt a materialist account of the structure of ideas discussed in chapter 2, which rests centrally on Marx's arguments in *The German Ideology* and in *Capital*.

Public opinion

In chapter 2, three central themes in opinion about state welfare were discussed. First a division between support for favoured mass services such as NHS, education, retirement pensions and provision for deserving groups (such as the disabled and the elderly) on the one hand, and suspicion of the unfavoured minority services such as unemployment or low-pay benefit and more general services unrelated to obvious need such as child benefit on the other. This theme seems stable over time and has been identified in a number of other surveys in this country and the USA in recent years.

The second theme concerned the ambivalence in public support between state and market welfare. To a considerable extent this seemed to relate to ideas about self-interest, although more general judgments about how society should be organised played a part. Thirdly, the pattern of opinion about welfare as it affected women's interests displayed a further ambivalence between a general ideological support for a family ethic with the consequent assumption that women had particular roles in caring for dependants, and considerable enthusiasm for state provision for dependent family members in detailed discussion of what should be available for various need groups.

The discussion of the weaknesses of survey data at the beginning of chapter 2 showed that such information is most useful as a general guide to the pattern of ideas in a society. Marx's account of 'commodity fetishism' provides a basis for the overall tendency to the individualism of interest. The point in essence is simple: the market system dominates the way in which we get access to many of the things we need. This system rests on the common understanding of things as commodities that are exclusively owned by individual people. This fact underlies the general ideological climate of individualism in capitalist societies.

The individualism of the market, to the extent that it is a dominant theme in apprehension of self-interest, has implications for people's understanding of political relations. The state stands against the dog-eat-dog self-interested anarchy of the market as an institution which unifies social relations by its monopoly of power in a given territory. The development of democratic forms of government suggests that the state can be organised to reflect a common or at least a majority interest against market chaos. Thus state and market stand opposed to each other. Marx argues consistently from his early critique of Hegel's approach to the state onwards (1975, pp. 87–9) that this led to an obscuring of the reality of the close links between the political and the economic. Just as market individualism glosses over the essential identity of interest of capital in the preservation of private property in the means of production, and its conflict with labour's interest in demolishing this, so democratic forms conceal the operation of the state in the interests of capital. Similarly proponents of laissez-faire wish to suggest that coalitions of interest in the market such as trade unions may bridge the politico-economic gulf to sway the state in a particular direction. However, here we are concerned with the similarity and common foundations of the economic and political conceptualisation of interests. The reality (from one perspective) of class in the market is inverted (from the perspective of market participants) to become a reality of individual interest. Similarly the reality of democratic state subject to market interest (from one perspective) becomes the inverted reality of the state that stands as a collective social force at an opposite pole to the individualism of the market (from another perspective).

How does this abstract theory relate to the pattern of public opinion about welfare services? The model leads in two directions which are consonant with popular ideas. These concern, on the one hand, coalitions of self-interest in the market and, on the other, ideas about the market system as a whole and the role of political intervention.

The strong popular support for the heartland of the welfare state, the big-spending mass services which are highly favoured across the population, is readily related to the consistent mass commodity interest in the provision of those services. Just as generalised attitudinal support for the welfare state as a whole relates most strongly to ideas about value for money (Taylor-Gooby, 1982, Table 8) so judgments about favoured services relate to ideas about need. This pattern contrasts with the minority unfavoured services which people are less likely to need and less likely to be prepared to pay taxes to support. In general support for the welfare state is a matter of self-interest defined by the dominant ideology of a society in which desired goods are bought and sold.

Clearly this explanation is not entirely satisfactory. Two problems exist. Firstly the pattern of mass-versus-minority services does not hold entirely true. Benefits for the sick and disabled, which are plausibly a minority interest yet receive mass support, and child benefit, a little favoured mass service, are the obvious counter-example. It may be speculated that value-judgments – about desert in the case of sick and disabled benefits and judgments about indiscriminate allocation in the case of child benefit – are relevant. It is not clear whether a commodity interest account that relates desert to exchange (as theoretical work on stigma does: Pinker, 1971, ch. 4) or concern at allocation because it is seen to redistribute from the mass of taxpayers (as Runciman's discussion of family allowance indicates: 1972, p. 266) is appropriate. The relevant data on opinions is not available.

The second problem concerns the role of more general value-judgments in influencing support. These are clearly significant, but play a relatively minor role compared to felt need (Taylor-Gooby, 1982). Thus, in general, it is possible to claim that commodities interest arguments provide the bedrock of understanding of the pattern of opinion between favoured and unfavoured provision.

The issue of ambivalence in opinion between market and state welfare may be related to the ideological status of these two institutions. On the one hand the individualism of the market provides the foundation for justification of private welfare provision. To the extent that commodity-exchange is the major system for meeting needs, it may be argued that the ideas associated with it become the prime ideas about how needs should be met. On the other hand individuals may see themselves as members of interest-groups which can use a democratic state to provide desired service to meet common needs – a kind of *ersatz* collectivism, founded on plurality of interest. The two roles of citizen in a democratic state and individual in the market provide the bases for different valued services. These are only in contradiction to the extent that market and state are seen to be in contradiction. Writers in the reformist tradition of whom the most important is Titmuss saw the welfare state as the use of state power to intervene in market inequalities (1974, pp. 29–30). However, if social policy is seen as a means of advancing shared private property interests that originate in the market, the conflict dissolves.

The third theme in popular ideas concerns women and the family. Again a variant of commodity interest can be used to explain ambivalence in ideas. The centrality of the commodity as the base of judgments of self-interest derives from the idea that the market is the main institution allocating resources to meet needs. The family also plays a role and the most important aspect of this is the use of unwaged women's labour to care for dependants (change the nappies), to process commodities into the form in which they are used (cook the beans) and to provide services (scrub the floor). A considerable body of research indicates that women bear a disproportionate share of the burden of these services even when they also work in paid employment (Oakley, 1981, p. 250; Rose, 1981, p. 503). In addition, the development of labour-saving devices does not seem to have a great impact on the amount of time spent in these services, although it may influence the nature of the work done. Current developments in the welfare state, particularly in the government commitment to community care, imply an increase in the burden of this work, which is likely to fall in the main on particular groups of women (see chapter 4).

The relationship between the family and the capitalist mode of production is much debated. It is arguable that family system fulfils material and ideological functions. On the one hand the existence of families enables the continuance of the working class at a lower level of wages than would otherwise be necessary, because unwaged women workers provide services in the home cheaper than they would cost in the market (Gardiner, 1977; McIntosh, 1979, p. 155). On the other hand, the family socialises people to fit into the existing system (Barrett, 1980, pp. 138–40). Both these suggestions may be challenged. Humphries in a controversial article argues that the working-class family is a base for resistance to capitalist oppression, as well as a site of additional exploitation (1977).

The argument for a simple functional link between families and capitalism is put in a nutshell by Deem:

> in most capitalist societies there remains a strong entrenched sexual division of labour separating what men do from what women do. Because of this it is both possible and feasible to argue that the sexual division of labour must be essential to the maintenance of capitalist society although the exact ways in which it is important . . . remain controversial (1978, p. 2).

This is simply a *non sequitur* in the absence of an unequivocal explanation of the origins and process of the functions.

The contemporary family form is not simply the product of the development of capitalism, whether or not certain aspects of it are helpful to that social system. The family provides a logically separate and independent system of meeting needs to the capitalist market although it is clearly integrated with it. This provides a base for the ethic of family ideology which emerges most strongly in the general statements about the appropriateness of state care for family dependants. In respect of particular services the emphasis is much more strongly on the individual, and the pattern of mass support for the favoured services for elderly dependants, and suspicion of minority childcare provision shows through. The pattern in this area is the result of the interaction of interests based on family provision and on market interests expressed through good value state services.

The central idea deployed in this account of the overall pattern of public opinion is of commodity fetishism. Clearly the structure of popular ideas is complex. People live in a market society and this makes them want large-scale collective services when these seem value for money; makes them support the market system at the same time in their role as market consumers; and produces a duality between this individualist structure of opinion and judgments based on a parallel family ethic. Appeal to these simple facts of everyday life goes a long way in explaining the structure of

115

popular ideas. The precise form in which these interests are realised and the ebb and flow of pressure between different groups with different alliances of interest differs according to myriad situational factors. However this general ideological foundation provides the bedrock on which the framework of welfare is constructed. The overall pattern is relatively stable over time. It constitutes a powerful reason why the seeds of current developments are to be found in the previous pattern of welfare rather than in sudden and critical change. At the same time it poses major obstacles to a substantial shift in the direction and in the consistent ambiguities of the welfare state.

Conclusion

The suggestion inherent in the argument of this chapter is that the traditions of discussion of ideology have exaggerated the size of the gulf between relativism and determinism. If the materialist thesis of ideas produced by social relations of production is interpreted with flexibility, space for the everyday experience of free will becomes available. From the viewpoint of commodity fetishism the assertion is not that all individuals in advanced capitalism must understand self-interest as exclusively individual and commodity based, nor that state and economy are invariably thought of as opposite and contradictory institutions. Rather it is that there is a natural tendency in people's thought to be concerned with meeting needs – natural, because people have real and impatient needs due to their existence in a natural world. If the prime way of meeting needs is through control over goods, and the main way of achieving this is through ownership and exchange in a private property system, then people will tend to think of self-interest within the bounds of individualism. There is no reason why they can't in principle take a longer view: it's just that the cards are stacked against it. Similarly the conceptual separation of state and market that results from a narrow commodity-centred view of the economic and thus the idea that there is no obstacle to the deployment of state power is not necessary – merely probable.

The position advanced here is in many ways analogous to the argument of Abercrombie, Hill and Turner (1980). The claim in that volume is that advocates of a 'dominant ideology thesis' in marxist social science are mistaken. The roots of Marx's account of social cohesion in class society are not to be found in the production of ideology in the interests of one class, but rather in what is termed the 'dull compulsion of economic relations'. This

tag is in fact quoted with approval thrice (pp. 57, 163 and 166).
Things are set up so that you have to work for pay: that's what
everyone does and to conceive of and struggle for a different social
order requires a huge effort against the present system.

> The advance of capitalist production develops a working-class
> which by education, tradition, habit, looks upon the conditions
> of that mode of production as self-evident laws of nature. The
> dull compulsion of economic relations completes the subjection
> of the labourer to the capitalist (Marx, 1974, p. 689).

It is the 'thereness' of social arrangements, the unalterability of
what is the case, that gives this world view its special force, that
elevates it to the status of common sense both in public opinion
and academic studies. The slope of ideas leads inexorably in this
direction. This is the basis of popular ideas, and of the success of
the new crisis theory. The virtue of this approach is that it chimes
in harmony with the dominant intellectual perspective of the
subject – reformism. It provides an analysis of the evident
weakness of the welfare state that does not undermine the central
tenet of reform – the state is in principle separate from market and
therefore in a position to radically upset market allocation of
goods.

Rudolph Klein in an influential paper (1980b) suggests that
social policy studies are threatened from two directions: first the
external crisis of the social and economic forces that challenge the
continued stability of the welfare state. We have argued that the
threat here does not result so much from a change in popular ideas
and democratic politics as from the inability of immobile arrangements to cope with social change. The second challenge is internal
and concerned with the growth of new theoretical orientations
which threaten to undermine the dominant reformist perspective
in the subject. The response of the main current of theory to this
challenge is instructive. Social policy writing moulds theoretical
challenges into a form in which they no longer confront the
assumption of reformism: the capacity of a capitalist state to
intervene in the market to achieve desired ends. This is further
evidence of the ideological power of that paradigm in the subject.
The ideas of intellectuals are no more immune from the power of
ideological structures than are those of ordinary citizens.

6

The crisis in welfare state studies

Once upon a time a valiant fellow had the idea that men were drowned in water only because they were possessed with the *idea of gravity*. If they were to knock this notion out of their heads . . . they would be sublimely proof against any danger from water. His whole life long he fought against the illusion of gravity, of whose harmful results all statistics brought him new and manifold evidence. This valiant fellow was the type of the new revolutionary philosopher . . .

Karl Marx and Frederick Engels *The German Ideology* 1970, p. 37

Marx is dead, Lenin is dead, and I'm not feeling too well myself!
West German Sponti Group Slogan

The argument of the book so far has been that the view that the welfare state is currently the victim of a sudden attack by the new right is somewhat misleading. There is no substantial shift in opinion against state welfare or for privatisation. The vision of the history of the welfare state as a decline from the golden age tends to mask the conflicts and continuities that have always existed in policy. The contemporary problems in the welfare state arise from the failure of policy to adapt to the demands of changing circumstances – from inertia rather than the radical development of policy. The question that follows is why new crisis theory should be influential, if it is incorrect. On the answer to this question turns any assessment of the future of the central academic standpoint in this area.

The dominant approach is fabian reformism. After a balmy youth as the commonsense of government in the Wilson era, this tradition has suffered sudden attack on three fronts. The success of reformism is challenged in the evidence that state welfare has not advanced equality; its popular appeal is overthrown by the 1979 and 1983 election victories; and the advent of feminist, marxist and liberal critiques of fabian theory demand a response. The capacity of the approach to handle empirical and political challenges depends ultimately on beating off the theoretical attack. In the empirical arena, reformism can only win back lost ground by showing that progress is feasible. This requires a reply to the theoretical claims that the welfare state is in principle irredeemably infected by patriarchy, capitalism or political serfdom. The political attack demands a practical strategy to win mass support for the welfare state. Reformism must counter theoretical arguments that the ideologies of family and private property or the tyranny of vested interests hold dominion in our society. Argument in empirical and political arenas is complex, fluid and subtle. Its success depends on victory at the theoretical level. In this chapter we focus on the response of social policy studies to the theoretical challenge.

Why is the new crisis theory plausible?

The problem to be faced in this section is that of why many academics have tended to see current events as implying greater changes in the politics of the welfare state than are justified. The answer is to be sought in the same structure of commodity fetishism and its application to ideas about state and market discussed in chapter 5, but this time viewed with the detachment of a commentator on society rather than a participant in it. The dominant tradition in social policy studies in the UK has been concerned exclusively with consumption – with the distribution of goods between people. Until recently its main area of interest was the market. Although consideration of allocation within households and families has recently developed this is almost entirely in terms of the deployment of commodities (Pahl, 1980; Zweig, 1961). Similarly, the operation of a voluntary sector alongside the market economy has been analysed as secondary.

If the dominant theme of social policy studies is commodity interests, the dominant strategy discussed is interventionist. The way to achieve desired allocations of goods is through state intervention in the market. In fact, for many writers this is a defining characteristic of the welfare state (Gough, 1979, p. 3; Briggs, 1972, and so on). Thus the two themes of fetishism – the basis of interest in individual command over commodities with the underlying principle of private property taken for granted; and the separation of state and economy – are the presumptions of the approach.

Within this overall framework various strands have developed. Of particular note is the egalitarian fabian tradition running from Tawney to Titmuss with its emphasis on market equality as the object of state intervention, and its investing of that equality with moral overtones to do with social integration. The elevation of the living standards of the group referred to by Townsend as 'the social minority' (1973) to those of the mass is not simply a question of the elimination of poverty but of the creation of a society in which all are united by participation in a common life-style. Thus, the often-misunderstood emphasis on life-style elements in Townsend's operationalisation of poverty (1979, ch. 6; see, for example, Piachaud's critique, 1981). The fabian approach to interventionism may be contrasted with social democratic ideals which are more concerned with the creation of a society in which inequalities are at least seen to be fair, and in which the use of policy to achieve economic efficiency plays a major role (Weale, 1983, p. 200). These strands in reformism have been extensively discussed elsewhere (see George and Wilding, 1976 or Taylor-Gooby and Dale, 1981, for example). Here we are concerned with the theory of crisis. It is writers in this tradition who tend to see current events as a crisis in the welfare state – a crisis of interventionism. This is because the alternative explanation – that current issues are simply the outcome of a democratic politics under particular circumstances in a society where certain ideas flourish (and have flourished) – cannot be thought through in a reformist framework. The problem for reformism is that such a central place for the role of ideology would make the whole reformist project of using state power to change economic relations implausible. The structure of ideas produced by market relations can always undermine that scheme. Implicit in the reformist project is the view that ideas are always subject to change by argument. This is contained in Keynes's oft-quoted dictum that 'nothing is mightier than an idea whose time has come', in Galbraith's assertion that 'the emancipation of belief is the most formidable of the tasks of reform and the one on which all else depends' (1973, p. 223) and in the whole political approach that used rational argument in order to change policy. If the structure of commodity interest is always stronger than the power of reformist ideas this approach has little future.

Three main strands in current thinking challenge the basic presumptions of the fabian tradition: that a democratic interventionist government can meet needs satisfactorily in a capitalist society. These are liberalism, feminism and marxism.

Liberalism

This refers to a range of approaches which stress a basic value of individual freedom and see the untrammelled operation of the market as the best way to realise that value. The seminal work of Friedman and Hayek has been extensively discussed in social policy writing in recent years (George and Wilding, 1976, ch. 2; Room, 1979; Taylor-Gooby and Dale, 1981, ch. 3; Bosanquet, 1983, chs 2 and 3) and the main points can be summarised briefly.

Friedman and Hayek share an individualism of method that directs their political economy. This is subject to pragmatic modification in the work of the former, and pushed to a logical limit by the latter. The principle of the commodity – that things should be exclusively owned and controlled by individuals – is an unargued assumption. Government intervention becomes coercion – unjustified interference with people's freedom to do what they like with what they happen to own. The analysis is directed by its starting-point, so that the case for an intervention in the market must be argued uphill, against the weight of the assumption that unfettered control by owners is the central virtue of society. Gamble develops the anti-democratic implications of the thesis of the sacrosanctity of commodity-ownership against political decisions (1979).

The assertion that the welfare state cannot attain the goal of enhancing human welfare because it is in principle ridden with vested interests, has in recent years been reinforced by the work of the 'public choice' school of economics, emanating mainly from the USA. Four defects with the operation of democratic interventionism are detected. First the problem of 'fiscal illusion': Buchanan (1952, 1963) draws on Puviani's point (1897) that the financing of state policies tends to derive from a general tax fund rather than earmarked taxes. This obscures the relation between tax payment and public expenditure. The combination of inflation and rising real incomes in post-war years have meant that real increases in tax revenues have been relatively painless. This has certainly been seen as a major cause of the expansion of welfare by a number of authors (Klein, 1976). In addition, as Mueller points out, (1979, p. 86), the existence of a 'fiscal illusion' tends to exaggerate the effect of some of the inherent problems of representative democracy that have been extensively analysed by students of voting. This forms the second area of defect of public choice theorists.

Four issues are of greatest significance. First the 'paradox of voting' discovered by Condorcet (1785) and made the centrepiece of Riker's elegantly argued text (1982). The point may be stated simply: suppose three people have three different preference orders for a bundle of policy options: the first prefers x to y and y to z; the second y to z and z to x; and the preference order of the third runs zxy. If we attempt to calculate the majority preference order we can find 2 to 1 majorities for the three preferences x over y (first and third voters versus the second); y over z (first and second versus the third) and z over x (second and third versus the first). The paradox is that although each individual's ordering is transitive, stating an unambiguous ordering of relative preference for each policy, the combined order is not. Depending on which policy we consider first we have exactly equal grounds for claiming that collective preference runs xyzx; yzxy or zxyz. In other words majority voting on a multiplicity of issues can easily produce ambiguous results: the outcome may well depend on the order in which the issues are presented.

It can be demonstrated that it is only in circumstances in which everyone ranges preferences along a single dimension (such as level of expenditure) that a single outcome of majority voting is guaranteed (Mueller, 1979, p. 41). However, preferences on welfare issues are often more complex (community care; residential provision; social care insurance or mixtures of all three?) and this casts doubt on the viability of simple democratic choice mechanisms. Can a policy-making apparatus of the usual democratic kind represent popular preferences faithfully?

The second issue of voting concerns the issue of vote-trading. If two people or interest groups each stand to benefit from different parts of two different packages of policy measures, it makes sense for them to combine forces to vote both through a committee, although other parts of the packages may be mildly against their own and strongly against other people's interests. Tullock is able to show that because majority voting measures number of supporters rather than intensity of preference it can lead to the approval of policies that actually have a negative effect on the community as a whole (1976). Riker is able to produce a number of examples of this process in action (1982, pp. 145–68).

These defects of majority decision-making procedures together with the observation that political parties which wish to appeal to the majority in a plural society will tend to offer a judicious mixture of policies as a package deal, some of which are bound to offend somebody (Breton, 1974, p. 50), undermines the claim of representative democracy to express the popular will. The third and fourth issues concern problems in the operation of democratic governments.

Bartlett (1973, ch. 9) and Judge and Hampson (1980) draw attention to the capacity of interest groups, political parties and governments to influence the decisions of the electorate by the supply of information. The effect is analogous to that of advertising in the commodity market. The persuasive messages of politicians are extensively analysed and widely discounted (Glasgow Media Group, 1976 and 1978; Golding and Middleton, 1982, ch. 7). However, many groups have strong interests in the area of welfare and are concerned to apply political pressure (Beer, 1966; Eckstein, 1960). The provision of information through reports, media interviews, case-studies giving evidence to official enquiries and commissions and informal contact with politicians is widespread.

The fourth issue concerns the operation of public bureaucracies. Niskanen argues that bureaucracies tend to expand above the optimum size because the control that the bureau has over information about its own activities and the level of need for them gives it a powerful lever in the extraction of funds from a sponsor. An additional reason is that the reward system and goals of the worker tend to be linked to the size of the bureau rather than the interests of the public (1971).

The individualism of Hayek and Friedman and the critique of the failings of representative democratic institutions have been linked together by a number of writers. A powerful example is Riker, who links a sophisticated theory of the aggregation of individual choice to an analysis of individual voting to defend liberal interpretations of democracy against populist ones. Populism as exemplified in the work of MacPherson argues that 'the opinions of the majority *must* be right and *must* be respected because the will of the people is the liberty of the people. In the liberal interpretation, there is no such magical identification. The outcome of voting is just a decision, and has no special moral character' (p. 14).

The conclusion of the book at a political level is the desirability of the restriction of the power of elected representatives through a multi-cameral legislation, a division between the legislative and the executive and between national and local government, an independent judiciary and limitations on tenure – in short Madisonian checks and balances (p. 250). At the normative level the disasters of the operation of competitive markets are judged less severe than those of the uncontrolled action of governments: 'losses of roughly the same scale are worse in a political context than an economic context. For both individual citizens and the whole society, losing a war and being pillaged, harried and murdered is worse than chronic unemployment and poverty' (p. 202). This judgment is, of course, open to question. Its net effect is to bastion the market against the scope of state intervention on grounds which parallel Hayek's: to allow the state access may promise many benefits in the short term, but it is to set one's foot on the slippery slope that can culminate in the absolute disaster of serfdom. A penny-plain version of the argument is found in many of the publications of the Institute of Economic Affairs, for example, Seldon (1981).

The general tenor of these arguments is to maintain that for a number of reasons, some to do with the nature of liberty and some to do with that of political institutions, the welfare state cannot enhance welfare. This constitutes a radical attack on the possibility of a welfare state. A recent strand in writing on social policy that seems likely to become influential in the future turns the edge of these arguments while accepting many of their premises.

The mixed economy of welfare

The phrase 'mixed economy of welfare' refers to the fact that the total welfare situation of any individual is the outcome of the combination of a wide variety of factors including the operation of state, market, voluntary and family provision. Attention is focussed on the interaction of all these bearers of benefit and not simply the state. This approach has received a great deal of attention in the early 1980s as the previous fabian orthodoxy weakened and has become the focus of a number of texts (Judge et al., 1983; Weale, 1983), has influenced others (Hadley and Hatch, 1981; Bosanquet, 1983) and has provided the theme for the 1983 Social Administration Association conference. In some ways it continues the concern of mainstream fabianism with the social division of welfare (Titmuss, 1955; Sinfield, 1978). The overall framework provides rich opportunities for individual exponents to vary the emphases between different aspects. One influential argument enables the potential and duty of interventionist democracies to achieve welfare to be restated. This is of interest because it starts out from individualist premises which are similar to those of Hayek and Friedman. In short it enables liberalist approaches to be incorporated within welfare statism.

The argument of Weale's text (1983) provides three foundations for a liberal theory of state intervention: the starting point is identical to that of Friedman (1966): a presumption in favour of individual autonomy. The theory is developed with reference to contractarian accounts of social choice. The third aspect of theory is the desirability of political participation.

The establishment of individual autonomy is seen as requiring on the one hand the familiar set of legal and political freedoms associated with western democracy. Indeed Friedman, Nozick (1971) and other laissez-faire liberals have seen such rights as part of the legitimate role of a minimal state. On the other hand, autonomy demands freedom from economic insecurity and the freedom to make deliberative life-plans (Weale, 1983, p. 54). The reasoning has parallels with that of Lukes (1976) and Plant (1980). In a society in which the market is a major allocator of resources, a limited measure of income maintenance is a necessary precondition of freedom: as Goodin (1982) suggests the notion of freedom has a dual aspect. Freedom is freedom *from* restraints *to* achieve goals, and autonomy implies the prerequisites for its exercise. In practice this suggests a radical redistribution of property rights and genuine equality of educational opportunity. It is important to note that Weale regards the principle of private property as 'the foundation of individual freedom and autonomy' (p. 63). The argument is that people need some control over property in order to be able to express themselves. Moreover, property presents a bulwark against the excesses of state planning – a claim which echoes Hayek. Thus the argument sets strict limits to how far redistribution may go and denies any suggestion of common property. It bears a close resemblance to its individualist antecedents. In addition, this degree of state intervention is not based on normative arguments about the nature of human need in the manner of Plant or Lukes. The argument returns to autonomy. The claim is that all citizens will themselves freely recognise the desirability of these restrictions on liberty, in order to make wider conditions of liberty available to all.

This argument has an obvious basis in Rawls's conception of collective choice in a situation where vested interests are set to one side. The second stage of the theory builds on this approach. Rawls argued that the basic rules of social justice could be deduced in a non-dictatorial manner by imagining the rules that people would set down for the apportionment of social rewards and disadvantages between social roles if they did not know which roles they would themselves occupy. Decisions made behind the 'veil of ignorance' cannot be biased since people cannot know how their judgments will affect their own eventual position. Yet they will have a strong interest in ensuring that social organisation is just in case they come to occupy an unfairly penalised position (Rawls, 1972, pp. 136–60).

Rawls concluded that the kind of caution which would prevail behind the veil of ignorance would make two rules for social organisation rational choices: the most extensive basic liberty for each which is compatible with a similar liberty for others; and the distribution of social and economic inequalities so that they are to the advantage of all (p. 60). The first principle is similar to the first foundation of state welfare in Weale's argument. The second justifies inequalities which might be expected to produce material growth: work incentives, rewards for risk-taking and entre-preneurship, extra advantages for mutually beneficial discovery, in short everything from company cars to non-progressive income tax. However, the inegalitarian impact of such policies is substan-tially weakened in Weale's account by appeal to 'risk aversion'. Unlike Rawls, Weale suggests that there are certain miseries which many people might wish to avoid so strongly that they would be willing to make sacrifices in economic growth in order to do so: need for health care or social security are important instances. Thus it is reasonable to suppose a legitimate role for the state in ensuring specific egalitarianism in these areas. A theory which rests on a sophisticated account of individual liberty has by now justified the greater part of the welfare state.

The third part of the theory concerns the likely development of policy in representative democracies. Weale takes the criticism of democratic institutions into account and strongly favours the construction of a system of checks and balances to limit the play of populism. However, unlike Riker, he does not suggest that the operation of political power leads to more disastrous results than that of free markets. In any case it is not clear that a system of private provision with a minimal state will advance individual autonomy to a greater extent than does interventionism. Indeed, the thrust of the first two stages of argument is to maintain that interventionism is likely to be strongly favoured by autonomous citizens. The upshot is the suggestion that the interplay of political participation will lead to complex and unpredicted results. However, it is likely that this process will generate further justifications for collective provision, through the sentiment of altruism as much as through the machination of self-interested groups.

In this argument, Weale follows the path of individualism. He focusses on consumption and on the legitimation of state intervention in capitalist markets in order to secure greater equalities in who gets what. His final claims about altruism regenerate the fabian interlinking of inequality with damage to social solidarity. The political process is seen as a more robust road to community than social choice theorists who operate in terms of a principle of self interest belief. The major features of the fabian approach are restated, deduced from liberal premises: the individualist critique of welfare statism is successfully incorporated. The point is that this approach is far more successful among the social administration community than alternative responses to the liberal challenge, which rely on attempting to take on the basis premises of methodological individualism head-on.

These arguments are representative of the move to incorporate liberalism in the defence of the welfare state. A critical challenge from a completely different direction is provided by feminism.

The challenge of feminist work

The explosion of feminist work has affected every aspect of social science from the late 1960s onwards. Writing in the general area of the exploration of the relation of women and society constitutes the largest single area of output and the most rapidly growing. This development is heavily influenced by the struggles of the women's movement. Here we confine attention to the relevance of this work to social policy. Does feminist writing constitute a radical challenge to the fabian approach to the welfare state? Has that challenge been successfully incorporated in the progress of the subject?

The rapid growth of feminist work and its topical and direct concerns pose problems to those who seek to divide the area into the categories of a theoretical framework. Here we draw on the argument developed in chapters 3 and 4 that the relevance of the welfare state for women is primarily through the family, and through consideration of the influence of policy on the roles of women as dependants and carers. This may lead to less emphasis on the role of women in the labour market, where they face oppressions that are additional to the class oppressions of men and which have been the subject of limited state action in the Equal Pay Act (1970) and the Sex Discrimination Act (1975). However, a family emphasis is justified for two reasons. First, to a great extent it is the role of women in the family that both legitimates and conditions their limited role in the labour market. The assumed availability of breadwinners with family wages explains low pay and the demands of family care make women more vulnerable to segregation (Reid and Wormald, 1982, pp. 147–56, 169–74). These assumptions feed through into the goals of women in education and are an important factor in explaining girls' subject orientation, which tends not to qualify them for higher paid work (McRobbie, 1974). At the same time, the failure of Equal Pay legislation has been primarily because it does not take these unequal demands into account. The legislation attempts to compel employers to pay equal wages for equal work and ignores the forces that tend to limit women to particular segments of the job market (Oakley, 1981, pp. 35–8).

Marxist feminist approaches may be divided into three loose categories: those that operate in a functionalist problematic, those that put the main emphasis on ideology, and those that place a greater stress on class. Functionalism poses many theoretical problems which have been extensively discussed elsewhere (see Carrier and Kendal, 1973 for example). In particular, it may imply a determinism if it is assumed that because B depends on A, this is a sufficient reason for A to be as it is. Secondly, its value as explanation is limited: if the determinism of the necessary link is rejected, functionalism tells us nothing about how things could be otherwise and consequently nothing about why they happen to be as they are. Nevertheless, functionalist approaches may be defended as a stage in the development of social analysis: once the functional relation has been described, alternative historical and circumstantial analyses which are logically independent of the functionalist account, may be developed to explain whys and wherefores. This strategy is common in marxist theory (Gough, 1979, p. 56; Cohen, 1978, pp. 285–6; Wolpe, 1978, p. 293).

Mary McIntosh (1979; 1978, p. 281) has played an important part in developing and defending such functional analyses of the role of the family in capitalist society. The argument seeks to demonstrate that the role of the state in contemporary capitalist society in reinforcing the power of men over women is indirect: 'through its support for a specific form of household: the family household dependent largely upon a male wage and upon female domestic servicing' (1978, p. 255). The central concept employed is that of 'reproduction'. In general all social processes cannot persist over time unless their conditions of existence are continually renewed. In the case of the capitalist labour process this applies to both the forces and the relations of production. The family contributes to both areas – producing human beings who are well-socialised and healthy and thus willing and able to play their part in the sphere of work. In addition, the condition of the family means that married women can be available to provide cheap work when needed, but are sustained by their dependence on husband-breadwinners when unnecessary. This 'reserve army of labour' helps to hold down overall wages, and to compensate for the fluctuations in economic cycles.

The state seeks to perpetuate these social arrangements by a number of processes: the organisation of social security denies married women benefits in their own right and construes them as dependants of husbands. Provision for one-parent families is limited and unsatisfactory. The organisation of child care, care for the elderly and home help services assumes the primary responsibility of the dependent housewife for these tasks. A range of services in education and social work exists to police and correct child-rearing practices. Thus government policy can be understood in terms of its role in defining the family in such a way that it continues to supply the needs of capitalism. 'It must be frankly admitted . . . that this formulation leads to an analysis that is functionalist in character' (p. 260). The stress on ideology in variants of this approach mitigates this problem.

Ginsburg, in a detailed historical analysis of social security and housing policy, rests his approach on Marx's account of the way capitalist social relations tend to produce their own sustaining ideology: because people meet their needs through commodity relations this tends to lead them to identify their interests as individuals, in terms of the amount of goods they can succeed in commanding, and to direct attention away from the social aspects of production and consumption (1979, ch. 1). This ideology percolates through to the family. It is a constant damper in the development of class consciousness and struggle and buttresses the system wherein people seek to enhance their own command over resources. A corresponding ideology can be traced from Engels's argument that the production and reproduction of life has a twofold character: on the one hand the production of the means of existence, on the other that of human beings themselves (1972, p. 71). From this flows, on the one hand, the division of labour in employment and class society, on the other, the division of labour in the family and the oppression of women. Ginsburg argues that, just as capitalism produces its own confusing ideology that substitutes individual for class relations, so patriarchy substitutes the individual roles of women and men in the family for a realisation of the collective subordination of all women to all men. This ideology justifies the policies of the state that assume the dependency and work of women in the family, and leads directly to the production of ideas which make possible the policies which are functional to capitalism. Thus an ideological approach can be complementary to a functionalist one.

Wilson also suggests that ideology is of central significance: 'reflecting the needs of capitalism as it developed, it (the Welfare State) also responded to the demands of the organised working class. These two contradictory forces acting upon welfare legislation are themselves influenced or distorted by the ideological components always present' (1977, p. 27). Yet here ideology means something rather different. The emphasis is on ideas coming from the top down, rather than rooted in the life experience of ordinary people. Ideology 'stamps the welfare state with attitudes repressive both to women and the poor' (p. 27). The struggle of ideas is between ideologies favouring different groups, and consciously produced by them, rather than between the partial ideas that life in a particular social set-up fosters and more complete alternatives.

The third feminist approach to social policy stresses the category of class. In an important book on the relationship between women's biology and women's subordination Sayers argues that 'sexual inequality has been determined directly by biological as well as social and historical factors' (1982, pp. 3–4). Her analysis of various arguments used to justify the inferior status and opportunities of women, derived from a concern that equality would damage women's reproductive capacity, from Social Darwinism, from socio-biological accounts of the natural origins of social relations and from claims about inmate male dominance and superior intellect, stresses the contribution of class differences to the impact of discrimination on women. For example, arguments about the implications of allegedly demanding male occupations for the more delicate constitutions of women have been used among the middle class to justify their exclusion from work in certain educational institutions and from highly paid professions. For working-class women, the main impact of argument from biological hazard has been to bar them from relatively highly paid manual work that involves contacts with toxins or with strenuous working conditions. The alternative strategy – that the professions should reorganise themselves to fit the needs of women and that industry should bear the responsibility (and cost) of controlling pollutants – is not pursued. 'Where such implications are spelt out, those advancing these apparently purely biological arguments have had to admit their primary motive in adducing them – namely, that of protecting their economic interest' (p. 25). This is a class-as well as a gender-based interest. Similarly, women were excluded from the prestigious occupation of airline pilot before the Second World War on the grounds that menstruation made them unreliable and more prone to accidents. Conversely, the claim that menstruation had no debilitating effects was later used to deny wartime women factory workers paid leave on account of menstrual symptoms. The social construction of menstruation varies in order to reinforce the class order of male society (pp. 120–2).

Sayers attacks liberal and radical versions of feminism which seek to deny the significance of biological differences between women and men because these are often used to justify oppression of women. Her point is that the way society deals with these differences can be two-edged. The crucial issue is whether treatment founded on alleged biological differences reinforces or weakens class inequalities: 'capitalism . . . has had to be fought every inch of the way to get it to concede equal rights to women, and to get real improvements in the condition of women – in . . . the family, in health care and at work' (p. 201). A major arena of this struggle is in the social construction of femininity in the welfare state. Here an important issue is the difference between the dependent status of working-class and middle-class women, who have access to greater resources for domestic labour and to more interesting work opportunities. The political implication is that action through the state is desirable to challenge the class inequalities as well as the subordination of women in the family.

These three approaches by marxists to the relation of state policy and the family stress the way in which women's position is functional to capitalism, is buttressed by the dominant ideology and is reinforced by its articulation with social class position. The radical perspective concentrates more on the direct relation between men and women in the role of woman as wife.

The central thrust of this approach is an analysis of sex as the basic social division in terms more or less analogous to the marxist account of social class. The relation between husband and wife in marriage becomes one of oppression and exploitation and the role of the state in reinforcing this dominion is the basis of a critique of social policy. Millett, for example, argues that the power of men over women amounts to 'the fundamental political division in our society'. It is 'more rigorous than class stratification, more uniform and more enduring'. Class divisions are of secondary importance to any account of women's social position: 'economic dependency renders her affiliations with any class a tangential, vicarious and temporary matter' (1971, p. 38). Firestone roots a similar claim to the analytical primacy of sex over class in biological reproduction. In a paraphrase of Marx (1859) she writes:

> The sexual-reproductive organisation of society always furnishes the real basis, starting from which we can alone work out the ultimate explanation of the whole superstructure of economic, juridical and political institutions as well as the religious, philosophical and other ideas of a given historical period (1972, p. 21).

Spot the difference! The theoretical dependence of family organisation on the economic in classical marxism is reversed.

The analysis leads directly to a politics of 'feminist revolution' in which the biological and cultural distinctiveness of women is celebrated and male supremacy directly confronted. These theories have been well-criticised by Barrett (1980, p. 12) and Sayers (1982, p. 187) as simplistic and reductionist. Sayers in particular stresses the circularity in the derivation of all forms of social inequality from biological differences while at the same time claiming to found a superior social order in precisely those differences of biology.

The work of Delphy has been influential because it attempts a more sophisticated account of the social construction of biological differences into a mechanism of oppression. Delphy links women's class position to the institution of marriage: the empirical evidence of the abrupt fall in living standards of most women when their marriage ends demonstrates that their economic position derives from dependence on men. Without this dependence their situation is essentially proletarian. In the marriage contract the husband extracts unpaid labour from the wife through a patriarchal rather than a capitalist mode of exploitation. Evidence of the role of the unpaid labour of wives in French agriculture is deployed to reinforce this argument, but no further support for its significance in industrial society is given (1977). The advance of this position is that it assigns women's work in the house a position of analytical independence and co-existence with wage-labour in capitalist industry. However, the details of the relation between the two remain shadowy. The role of state policy is little analysed by Delphy. However, it seems feasible to suggest that, just as many marxists have given accounts of the way in which the administration of social security reinforces work incentives and maintains the workforce when it is unable to work (Kincaid, 1975, p. 221;

Gough, 1979, p. 45), so an additional and separate role of policy would be to maintain patriarchal exploitation in the home. The lack of official support or collective substitution for housework in day nurseries, communal laundry and restaurant facilities, the assumptions of dependency, and the failure to ensure comparable wages in work are all possible aspects of this process. Nonetheless, it is unnecessary to provide a separate account of housework in order to explain these phenomena. As marxist feminists suggest, the way policy treats housework can be understood more economically in terms of accounts of reproduction in capitalist labour systems (Barrett and McIntosh, 1980). The argument that women constitute a class, with a common situation so powerful that it transcends all differences of relation to conventional social classes, is shared by all these approaches. As Sayers argues, it diverts attention from real differences in the lives of women of different classes, differences that extend to the way woman's common biology is treated by society.

What are the implications of the variety of feminist approaches to state and family for work on social policy? The first point is that a great deal of the feminist work on the nuts and bolts of welfare state activity tends to be eclectic and fails to fit the categories sketched out above neatly. A good example is provided by Rose's discussion of the work of Titmuss. The strengths of Titmuss's approach are characterised as 'an innovative methodology and a coherent social theory' (1981, p. 479). The methodology stresses the importance of a holistic view of social relations which extends beyond state and market to include voluntary action, and, Rose argues, the family. The social theory involves the conception of a society 'integrated through a redistributive social policy which facilitates the growth of altruism' – the realisation of which is socialism (p. 482). It is the scope and precision of this approach which is important. The Titmuss paradigm with its insistence on the intimate and the concrete refuses to dissolve the specificity of women's oppression into the sex-blind categories of the 'new' political economy (p. 501). The outcome is on the one hand strong support for the 'new found political economy of welfare' with its marxist foundations, and on the other concern 'while this new work . . . richly conceives of welfare as a totality within the accumulation and legitimation process, it also threatens to lose the possibility of integrating the analysis of capitalism with that of the household/family . . .' (p. 495). This requires the vision of the good society, and the painstaking attention to detail of the fabian tradition of empirical work. Here and elsewhere (see Rose and Rose, 1982) the theoretical world is feminist/marxist. The insistence on the analytical independence of the family form lies in uneasy relation to this, and is closer to the radical feminist tradition.

Stress on the role of the state in the construction of the family and of the role of women within it leads to a clear challenge to fabianism in some variants. Functionalist marxism implies that certain family forms are necessary props to capitalism. Their removal does not appear on the political agenda of a capitalist society. Radical feminism is on even stronger ground in its argument. If women's subordination is a common feature of all societies and if the struggle centres on basic facts of biology, attempts to reform minor aspects of state policy become an irrelevance. The interesting point is that these approaches are virtually ignored within the mainstream of current social policy writing. Rose's essay referred to above is a good example of a marxist feminism which emphasises the importance of 'the painstaking documentation of inequalities in the relations of distribution' (p. 501) and the retention of the broad outlines of the fabian tradition.

Sayers discusses the activities of liberal feminists who are concerned to achieve equal rights for women without analysing the relationship between women's oppression and the organisation of capitalist society (1982, p. 175). This strand is strongly evident in much social policy writing. It is closely analogous to fabianism both in its stress on individual inequalities of consumption and outcome, and in its assumption that the exposure of injustice is likely to lead to political change. A good example is Finch and Groves's careful demonstration that community care policies operate in a way that is oppressive of women. They conclude:

> The onus is on any government which leaves equal opportunities legislation on the statute book to demonstrate that the pro-motion of equal opportunities is a commitment which pervades all policies, including those relating to community care. Without that intention, equal opportunities legislation represents nothing more than pious hypocrisy (1980, p. 511).

Land has provided a comparable analysis of the assumptions lying behind social security in a number of influential articles (1976, 1978).

The consistency of policy over time gives support to the view that powerful interests lie behind it. However, the sophisticated analysis of the apparatus of oppression is not matched by an equally sophisticated analysis of the process of change. The assumption is that reason by itself has political force. This embodies the idealist assertion of the primacy of spirit that underlies fabianism.

The social policy tradition turns the challenge of feminism by selecting out those feminist approaches which offer the least radical threat to its presumptions. Thus reformism with its assumption of the primacy of the political over the economic and the feasibility of state-based reforms remains the dominant approach. A similar development may be discerned in the incorporation of marxism.

The challenge of marxism

Marxist-inspired critiques of the welfare state have become increasingly important in the 1970s. They have built on the rapid development of marxist work in social science in recent years, and in particular on the considerable attention which has been paid to the analysis of the state. In this section we will review the two main themes in this work, and seek to show that the approach which is most amenable to adaptation and incorporation is the one which has been most frequently discussed in the social policy literature, to the extent that the alternative is virtually ignored.

Since marxist work is directed at social change, the central question in analysis of the state concerns the extent to which state power limits the achievement of socialism. To what extent is it possible to change, modify or reform state policy in a capitalist society? If the state is ultimately under the power of capital there are strict limits to the capacity of political pressure to reform it and the fabian thesis must be rejected. If on the other hand there is space for manoeuvre, and that space is understood in such a way that a vigorous, conscious and determined working class can create a welfare policy that does unambiguously serve their interests, then marxism and fabianism occupy positions on a continuum.

If the simplicities of conspiracy theory (which models the working of society as a whole on Oxbridge entrance or Lloyd's of London) are ignored, accounts of the relation of capital and the state can conveniently be approached through the much-discussed notion of 'relative autonomy'. What is the degree of freedom of capital from the state and what are its limits? Current marxist work provides two kinds of answers, resting on notions of class and ideology respectively.

The class theoretic approach is well summarised in the influential work of Miliband. The central point of his 'analysis of the western system of power' is an assertion of the dominance of class-cleavages against the pluralist democratic view of society which is 'in all essentials wrong' (1973, p. 6). He asserts three basic reasons for the dominance of the capitalist class. First, a particular group controls central institutions: it is a 'basic fact of life in advanced capitalist societies that the vast majority . . . has been governed, represented, administered, judged and commanded in war by people drawn from other economically and socially superior and relatively distant classes' (p. 62). The second point is 'the commitment which governments . . . have to the private enter-prise system . . . its economic rationality enormously limits their freedom of action' (p. 71). Third, there is the role of ideology and this is characterised as a conscious and persistent activity of the capitalist class:

> the subordinate classes . . . have to be persuaded to accept the existing social order and to confine their demands and aspir-ations within its limits. For dominant groups, there can be no enterprise of greater importance, and there is none which requires greater exertion on a continuous basis, since the battle is never finally won (p. 160).

In more recent work Miliband repeats substantially similar arguments: the state leans towards the interests of capital because of 'the character of its leading personnel, the pressures exerted by the economically dominant class and the structural constraints imposed by the mode of production' (1978, p. 74; see also 1982, p. 95).

This approach characterises the State as a territory which is at present occupied by a particular class. There is no reason (in principle) why another class should not be able to displace it. The analysis in parallel to Stuart Hall's account of the rise of the radical right: 'it has to be understood in direct relation to alternative political formations attempting to occupy and command the same space' (1979, p. 18). Class-struggle over the state is directly analogous to political struggle in any institution. This weakens the distinction between marxism and any pluralist theory of power-blocs or interest-groups dangerously.

In the development of marxist account of social policy, a second element has been added to the notion of the state as a neutral battle ground between classes. This derives from the political economy of O'Connor re-worked by Gough. O'Connor presents a theory of the contradictions of advanced capitalist societies which has strong functionalist overtones. The basic point is that a capitalist state must fulfil a number of functions of which two are of most importance – accumulation, or the provision of the wherewithal in infrastructure, communications, skilled labour and so on to help capital make profits; and legitimation – the social control aspects which figure largely in social policy (1973, pp. 7–12). Many other writers have made similar points (for example Galbraith, 1967, chs 4, 5, 21). O'Connor's important contribution is the argument that in modern societies the simultaneous fulfilment of these needs presents insuperable problems. The costs of securing profits and social harmony spiral as developed capitalism requires an ever-more sophisticated workforce and infrastructure, and more evidence of equality of opportunity and social compensation for diswelfare. At the same time there is no intrinsic reason why people should be prepared to pay more in taxes to finance them. While Habermas has developed similar arguments to support the thesis of an inbuilt tendency to 'legitimation crisis' in advanced capitalist states (1975, pt. II), O'Connor suggests a trend to fiscal crisis: a perennial 'tendency for state expenditures to increase more rapidly than the means of financing them' (p. 9).

O'Connor does not analyse the implications for the welfare state, although similar arguments lead other writers to suggest that the welfare state may only be a passing phase in the deployment by the ruling class of different themes in the repertoire of democratic capitalism to secure popular support (Wolfe, 1979, ch. 7). The most significant development of the fiscal crisis thesis is in the work of Gough, who unites it to Miliband's account of relative autonomy.

In Gough's political economy, the pressures from labour and capital operating on the terrain of the state become the operational forces which generate O'Connor's 'fiscal crisis' tendency. This is worked out in an ingenious account of the development of public expenditure and of the stagflationary crisis in the UK. The relation between the welfare state and capital is discussed in terms of direct quotation from the work of Miliband (1979, pp. 42–3). O'Connor's work is presented as 'the most important marxist work in recent years' in the delineation of the functions of the state (p. 51). The role of Miliband's account of state politics as struggle is to provide a dynamic element to the functions it performs. The answer is that (so far) the capitalist class has won the struggle.

An alternative approach claims that in struggle over the state people's ideas are not free to be swayed in class struggle. Rather they are influenced by ideological strands which emerge from the social relations in which they engage. The dominant ideology gives a particular tendency to conceptions of interest and of legitimate government policy and this is what is most important in limiting the relative autonomy of the state. The balance of class forces discussed by other writers is an additional factor, but ideology is thrust to the centre of the stage and it is ideology that restricts the capacity of the working class to use the state against capital. Struggle in relation to the state is not analogous to other forms of struggle because it operates in a different framework of ideas.

The argument may be developed in two directions. Firstly an abstract theoretical approach rests heavily on the emphasis of some aspects of the work of Marx and Engels. The account of the 'fetishism of commodities' in *Capital*, Book I provides an explanation of how people tend to think about the way they relate to others. The point made is that production is a social process involving the interlinked activities of many people. Similarly the purchase and use of goods entwines the consumer in a social chain. However the chain is not obvious. In market capitalism what interests people is the price of goods, the wages paid to labour, the value of what is exchanged. The social character of production is obscured, to be replaced by individual relations of exchange of goods: 'a definite social relation between men . . . assumes in their eyes, the fantastic form of a relation between things' (Marx, 1974, p. 77). The outcome is that people's interests become individualised, opposed to those of other consumers or producers and the possibilities of collective action to change social processes are undermined. In relation to welfare, attention is focussed on the services and benefits you get and on how much you pay for them, not on the overall issues of redistribution and the pro- duction of the services and goods consumed.

The argument may be taken a stage further in consideration of the nature of the state. The development of market society has obscured the political character of economic forms which in previous societies was a matter of everyday experience: exploit- ation by lords or slave-owners was open and obvious in the power relations of the physical ownership of workers or in feudal rights over a portion of their work. In capitalism, exchange relations appear individual and equal and overt power is concentrated on the state. The development of political democracy ensures that the state expresses common or at least majority interests. The counterpart of a formally free and equal civil society was the separation of power and political institutions into the state, resting on free and equal suffrage (Marx, 1975, p. 90).

The outcome is that people pursue their interests in political organisation through government, but the crucial issue is that their interests are conceived in partial and limited ways in relation to commodities. If command over commodities is fundamental the basic principle of private property is necessarily unchallenged. The last stage in the argument is the assertion that it is precisely private property in the means of production which is responsible for class power in capitalist society. The implication for the welfare state is that the whole ideological bias of society militates against challenging this. The fundamental limit to the relative autonomy of the state springs from ideology, and ideology is generated not by the conscious actions of social actors but by the material relations in which they find themselves. Because they satisfy needs through commodities, they are apt to see the maintenance of the system of commodities as the legitimate role of government.

Ginsburg provides an empirical application of the approach. He analyses the capitalist state as an essential prop to the privatisation of interest because it 'maintains and reproduces the separation between the economic, apparently merely technical, relations of production and the "public" political relations of the democratic process' (1979, p. 37). The argument of the book stresses the role of class struggle in specific historical contexts. Within the overall framework of ideology, groups within the working-class realise collective interests and strive to attain them. The maintenance of policies which are not inimical to capitalism is a process requiring effort and the occasional shedding of blood. Its outcome is not a forgone conclusion:

> the working class has had to accept capitalist welfare as an immediate amelioration of its conditions of existence, though it has restricted the terms on which it is offered . . . means-testing, work relief, fair rents etc . . . This acceptance has been predicated on the hope that the working class would be able to impose its own values . . . this has only happened in a strictly limited fashion and only when it presents no threat to capital (p. 12).

The argument is worked out in a detailed account of the development of housing and social security policy and provides an empirical counterbalance to the weight of abstract theory.

A recent study by a group of scholars and activists extends the argument to analyse the experience of consumers of welfare services and welfare state workers. The starting point is the contradictions that teachers, council workers, the unemployed, NHS auxiliaries, public transport employees, find in everyday life. The state's provision is a good – it meets real needs, provides benefits and services for which there is no satisfactory alternative. Yet the way in which provision is made is unsatisfactory – bureaucrats control the conditions of benefit allocation, education is trammelled into sorting out children for jobs, local authority work for the community rests on the exploitation of low-waged workers. The central argument is that this oppression results from the way the state appears to stand apart from the exploitative relations of the market, yet simply 'casts a protective and opaque seal of freedom and equality over the class dominion of capitalism' (Edinburgh Weekend Return Group, 1979, p. 38). The fetishism of state relations obscures the real relation of state policy and capitalism. At the same time this ideological gloss is not invulnerable:

> the veneer of equality and harmony scarcely conceals the daily eruptions of state violence and discrimination . . . and the . . . sabotage, truancy, absenteeism, vandalism and the million other acts of rebellion which capital is constantly seeking to control or repress.

Both Ginsburg and the Edinburgh Group seek to articulate accounts of class struggle and the power of ideology into a flexible approach which will provide satisfactory accounts of the development and the experience of welfare. These are fundamentally different from the 'class-theoretic' approaches because they posit a structural force in ideology which limits the relative autonomy of the state.

Recent work in social policy studies is quite unambiguous in the way it bases itself on class approaches. Saville's widely quoted essay provides a good example of the social administration treatment of marxism. In this work, the welfare state is essentially a compromise in class struggle. However, this is discussed at the level of political controversy. It concludes

> since the welfare state in Britain developed within a mature capitalist society, with a ruling class long experienced and much skilled in the handling of public affairs, its growth . . . has been slow and controlled; and the central interests of private property have never seriously been challenged (1975, p. 69).

The ideological framework of class action does not enter into the detailed discussion of recent history.

Several writers present marxism in terms of a broad distinction between consensus and conflict theory (George and Wilding,

140

1984; Hall, Land, Parker and Webb, 1975; Hill, 1980; Rein, 1976).
The basic dichotomy is between those who see society as
characterised by a structure of inequalities and opposed interests
and those who do not. The framework sets class against pluralist
views in the tradition of Miliband. Marxism is the paradigmatic
conflict view and ideology is not seriously considered.

The dominance of Miliband's framework in major texts which
present marxist ideas to social policy students (Gough, 1979;
George and Wilding, 1976, ch. 5; Hall et al., 1975, pp. 152–3)
undermines serious consideration of the variants of marxism which
stress the role of ideology. Yet it is precisely these variants which
offer the strongest challenge to the fabian tradition, because they
imply that there are strict limits to the scope of reformism and the
capacity of the state to govern the market. The main line of social
policy studies, by emphasising particular strands in marxism, turns
a potential radical challenge, and returns to business as usual, with
a rather more comprehensive notion of interest group set forward
under the title 'social class'.

Conclusion

In this chapter, the three main challenges to the fabian orthodoxy
at a theoretical level have been discussed. Fabianism has a
remarkable capacity to incorporate these threats and thus avoid
the consequences of the intellectual crisis they imply. How does
this come about? The answer rests on the materialist analysis of
ideology in chapter 5: in market capitalism, reformism is common
sense. On the one hand, the market distribution of goods is the
natural and legitimate sphere of private property. On the other
hand, it makes sense for individuals to advance their several
market interests by coalition and the use of political power. What
the commonsense ideology of market society does not include is a
space for the recognition of social forces that undermine the
operation of this process. New right thinkers claim that the use of
state power will destroy the system for maximising liberty;
marxists argue that there are limits to state action springing from
class forces and ideology; feminists maintain that structures of
patriarchal power constrain the state. None of these approaches
can be thought about satisfactorily within reformism: all tend to be
ignored, and their bearers reduced to assertions that fit within the
fabian framework. This redirection of theoretical challenges
furnishes a further example of the importance of the ideology of

private property in influencing the ideas of intellectuals about state welfare.

The reclaiming of theoretical challenges is a general ideological tendency that underpins reformist thought. The identification of this process is something that does not contradict the possibility that intellectual strands opposed to reformism may arise. What it does suggest is that by and large they will not prosper. The same underlying tendency that equates mass perception of interest with private property and fosters the separation of state and market promotes an ambiguity in support for public and private welfare and a suspicion of the universal welfare state. It also nourishes the reformist perception of welfare as consumption controlled by state power over the market. These currents flow through popular and intellectual understanding of the welfare state. To make them flow in new channels requires a considerable and sustained effort. The message for those who see a contemporary crisis in the welfare state or an internal crisis in social policy studies is that of the *Hitchhiker's Guide to the Galaxy*: 'Don't Panic!' The forces that mould the status quo are still alive. For those who are concerned to achieve a redirection of welfare, to meet human needs rather than buttress the capitalist economy, class privilege and the family system, the task is bleak. The obstacles to reform lie in the assumptions and policies of the welfare state itself rather than in redirection by politicians. In the long term the struggle to alter these is against the pattern of ideas engendered by patriarchal capitalism itself – the old enemy, not the new right.

References

Abel-Smith, B. (1983), 'Assessing the balance-sheet', in Glennerster (ed.) (1983), *op. cit.*

Abercrombie, N., Hill, S. and Turner, B. (1980), *The Dominant Ideology Thesis*, London, Allen & Unwin.

Abrams, M. (1973), 'Subjective social indicators', in Central Statistical Office, *Social Trends*, 1973, London, HMSO.

Alt, J. (1979), *The Politics of Economic Decline*, Cambridge, Cambridge University Press.

Althusser, L. (1969), *For Marx*, London, Allen Lane.

Althusser, L. (1972), *Politics and History*, London, New Left Books.

Althusser, L. (1977), *Reading Capital* (2nd edition), London, New Left Books.

Anderson, P. (1977), 'The antinomies of Antonio Gramsci', *New Left Review*, no. 110, November 1976/January 1977.

Aristotle (1963), *The Poetics*, edited by R. Bambrough, London, Mentor.

Bacon, R. and Eltis, W. (1976), *Britain's Economic Problem: Too Few Producers*, London, Macmillan.

Barker, M. (1980), *The New Racism: the Conservatives and the Ideology of the Tribe*, London, Junction Books.

Barrett, M. (1980), *Women's Oppression Today*, London, Verso.

Barrett, M. and McIntosh, M. (1980), 'The family wage', *Capital and Class*, no. 11.

Bartlett, R. (1973), *Economic Foundations of Political Power*, New York, Free Press.

Beechey, V. (1977), 'Some notes on female wage labour in the capitalist mode of production', *Capital and Class*, 1977, no. 3.

Beer, S. (1969), *Modern British Politics*, London, Faber.

Beer, S. (1982), *Britain Against Itself*, London, Faber.

Bell, D. (1961), *The End of Ideology*, New York, Collier.

Berger, P. and Luckmann, T. (1966), *The Social Construction of Reality*, London, Allen Lane.

Berthoud, R., Brown, J. and Cooper, S. (1981), *Poverty and the Development of Anti-Poverty Policy in the UK*, London, Heinemann.

References

Beveridge, W. (1942), *Social Insurance and Allied Services* (Beveridge Report), Cmnd 6404, London, HMSO.

Birmingham Centre for Contemporary Cultural Studies (1982), *The Empire Strikes Back*, Birmingham University, Hutchinson.

Black Report (1982), *Inequalities in Health* (mimeo), London, DHSS.

Blake, W. (1927), *Poems and Prophecies*, London, Everyman.

Blanke, B., Jurgens, U. and Kastendick, H. (1978), 'On the Current Marxist Discussion on the Analysis of Form and Function of the Bourgeois State', in Holloway and Picciotto, *op. cit.*

Bosanquet, N. (1983), *After the New Right*, London, Heinemann.

Bradshaw, J. and Deacon, A. (1983), *Reserved for the Poor*, Oxford, Basil Blackwell.

Breton, A. (1974), *The Economic Theory of Representative Government*, Chicago, Aldine.

Breughel, I. (1979), 'Women as a reserve army of labour – a note on recent British experience', *The Feminist Review*, vol. 3, no. 1.

Briggs, A. (1972), 'The welfare state' in Schonfield, A. and Schottland, C. (eds), *The Modern State*, London, Oxford University Press.

Brittan, S. (1975), 'The economic contradictions of democracy', *British Journal of Political Science*, vol. 5, no. 1.

Buchanan, J. (1952), 'Federal grants and resource allocation', *Journal of Political Economy*, vol. 60, no. 2.

Buchanan, J. (1963), 'The economics of earmarked taxes', *Journal of Political Economy*, vol. 71, no. 3.

Bull, D. and Wilding, P. (1983), *Thatcherism and the Poor*, London, Child Poverty Action Group.

BUPA (1982), 'Provident Scheme Statistics, 1981' (mimeo), London, British United Patents Association.

Burghes, L. (1983), 'The new poor', *New Society*, 3 November 1983.

Butler, D. and Stokes, D. (1971), *Political Change in Britain* (2nd edition, 1974), London, Macmillan.

Butler, D. and Kavanagh, D. (1979), *The British General Election of 1979*, London, Macmillan.

Calder, A. (1969), *The People's War*, London, Cape.

Callinicos, A. (1976), *Althusser's Marxism*, London, Pluto.

Carrier, J. and Kendal, I. (1973), 'Social change and social policy', *Journal of Social Policy*, vol. 2, no. 3.

Carter, G., Fifield, J. and Shields, H. (1973), *Public Attitudes to Welfare*, California, University of South California Press.

Carver, T. (1982), *Marx's Social Theory*, Oxford, Oxford University Press.

Central Statistical Office (1980), *Social Trends*, no. 10, London, HMSO.

Central Statistical Office (1982), *Social Trends*, no. 12, London, HMSO.

Central Statistical Office (1983), *Social Trends*, no. 13, London, HMSO.

Central Statistical Office (1984), *Social Trends*, no. 14, London, HMSO.

Coates, K. (ed.) (1980), *What Went Wrong?* Nottingham, Spokesman.

Cohen, G. (1978), *Marx's Theory of History*, Oxford, Clarendon Press.

Condorcet, M. (1785), *Essai sur l'application de l'analyse à la probabilité des decisions rendues à la pluraliste des voix*, Paris.

Conservative Party (1979), *The Election Manifesto*, London, Conservative Central Office.

Cooke, F. (1979), *Who Should Be Helped?* New York, Sage.

Coote, A. and Campbell, B. (1982), *Sweet Freedom!* London, Pan.

Corrigan, P. (1979), 'Popular consciousness and social democracy', *Marxism Today*, December, 1979.

Coughlin, R. (1980), *Ideology, Public Opinion and Welfare Policy*, California, University of California Press.

Crewe, I. and Sarlvik, B. (1983), *Decade of Dealignment*, Cambridge, Cambridge University Press.

Crosland, A. (1976), *Socialism Now*, London, Cape.

Curtin, R. and Cowan, C. (1975), 'Public attitudes towards fiscal programmes', in Strumpel, B., Cowan, C., Justin, F., and Schmiedeskamp, J. (eds), *Surveys of Consumers*, Michigan, Institute for Social Research, University of Michigan.

Dahrendorf, R. (1980), 'Efficiency and effectiveness', *Political Quarterly*, vol. 51, no. 4.

Daniel, W. (1980), *Maternity Rights*, London, Policy Studies Institute, Report no. 588.

David, M. (1980), *The State, the Family and Education*, London, Routledge & Kegan Paul.

Davies, B. (in association with Reddin, M.) (1978), *University Selectivity and Effectiveness in Social Policy*, London, Heinemann.

Deacon, A. (1977), 'Scrounger bashing', *New Society*, 17 November 1977.

Deacon, A. (1978), 'The scrounging controversy: public attitudes towards the unemployed in contemporary Britain', *Social and Economic Administration*, vol. 12, no. 2.

Debray, R. (1973), *Prison Writings*, Harmondsworth, Penguin.

Deem, R. (1978), *Women and Schooling*, London, Routledge & Kegan Paul.

Deem, R. (1981), 'State policy and ideology in the education of women, 1944–80', *British Journal of the Sociology of Education*, vol. 2, no. 2.

Delphy, C. (1977), *The Main Enemy*, London, Women's Resources and Research Centre.

Department of Education and Science (1983), *Report by Her Majesty's Inspectors on the Effect of Local Authority Expenditure Policies on Education: 1982* (mimeo), London, Department of Education and Science.

Department of Employment (1981), 'Labour force outlook to 1986', *Department of Employment Gazette*, April 1981, London.

Department of Employment (1983), 'Statistical Series', *Department of Employment Gazette*, September 1983, London.

Department of the Environment (1983), *Housing and Construction Statistics, 1972–82*, London, Department of the Environment.

Department of Health and Social Security (1980), *Occupational Sick Pay*, Cmnd 7864, London, HMSO.

Donnison, D. (1979), 'Social welfare after Titmuss', *Journal of Social Policy*, vol. 8, no. 2.

Douglas, J. (1976), 'The overloaded crown', *British Journal of Political Science*, vol. 6, no. 4.

Downs, A. (1960), 'Why the government budget is too small in a democracy', *World Politics*, vol. 12, no. 3.

Downs, A. (1961), 'In defence of majority voting', *Journal of Political Economy*, vol. 69, no. 2.

Duke, V. and Edgell, S. (1981), *The Politics of the Cuts* (mimeo), final report to the Social Science Research Council.

Duke, V. and Edgell, S. (1983), 'Gender and social policy: the impact of public expenditure cuts', *Journal of Social Policy*, vol. 12, no. 3.

Dunleavy, P. (1979), 'The political implications of sectoral cleavages and the growth of state employment – parts I and II', *Political Studies*, vol. 28, nos 3 and 4.

Dunleavy, P. (1980), *Urban Political Analysis*, London, Macmillan.

Dunleavy, P. (1981), *The Politics of Mass Housing in Britain, 1945–75*, Oxford, Clarendon Press.

References

Durkheim, E. (1964), *The Rules of Sociological Method*, New York, Free Press.
Eckstein, H. (1960), *Pressure Group Politics: the Case of the British Medical Association*, London, Allen & Unwin.
Edinburgh Weekend Return Group (1979), *In and Against the State*, London, Edinburgh Weekend Return Group.
Engels, F. (1970), *Ludwig Feuerbach and the End of Classical German Philosophy*, in K. Marx and F. Engels, *Selected Works*, London, Lawrence & Wishart.
Engels, F. (1972), *The Origins of the Family, Private Property and the State*, New York, Pathfinders.
Feagin, J. (1975), *Subordinating the Poor*, New York, Prentice-Hall.
Feuerbach, L. (1957), *The Essence of Christianity*, New York, Harper & Row.
Field, F. (1981), *Inequality in Britain*, London, Fontana.
Fimister, G. (1983), 'Social security: extending the mass role', in Bull and Wilding, 1983, *op. cit.*
Finch, J. and Groves, D. (1980), 'Community care and the family: a case for equal opportunities?' *Journal of Social Policy*, vol. 9, no. 4.
Firestone, S. (1972), *The Dialectic of Sex*, London, Cape.
Fishbein, M., Thomas, K. and Jaccard, J. (1976), *Voting Behaviour in Britain* (mimeo), London, Social Science Research Council Survey Unit.
Fogarty, M. (1983), 'Pensions – politics and prospects', in Jones, C. and Stevenson, J. (eds), *The Year Book of Social Policy – 1982*, London, Routledge & Kegan Paul.
Forsyth, G. (1966), *Doctors and State Medicine*, London, Pitman.
Friedman, M. (1966), *Capitalism and Freedom*, Chicago, Chicago University Press.
Friedman, M. and R. (1980), *Free to Choose*, Harmondsworth, Penguin.
Fromm, E. (1963), *The Sane Society*, London, Routledge & Kegan Paul.
Galbraith, J. (1967), *The Affluent Society*, London, Hamish Hamilton.
Galbraith, J. (1973), *Economics and the Public Purpose*, New York, Houghton Mifflin.
Galbraith, J. (1977), *The Affluent Society*, New York, Hamish Hamilton.
Gamble, A. (1979), 'The free economy and the strong state', in Saville, J. and Miliband, R. (eds), *Socialist Register, 1979*, London, Merlin Press.
Gardiner, H. (1977), 'Women in the labour process', in Hunt, A. (ed.), *Class and Class Structures*, London, Lawrence & Wishart.
George, V. and Wilding, P. (1972), 'Social values, social class and social policy', *Social and Economic Administration*, vol. 6, no. 3.
George, V. and Wilding, P. (1984), *Ideology and Social Welfare* (first edition, 1976), London, Routledge & Kegan Paul.
Geras, N. (1972), 'Essence and appearance in Marx's *Capital*, in Blackburn R. (ed.), *Ideology in Social Science*, Harmondsworth, Penguin.
Ginsburg, N. (1979), *Class, Capital and Social Policy*, London, Macmillan.
Glasgow University Media Group (1976), *Bad News*, London, Routledge & Kegan Paul.
Glasgow University Media Group (1978), *More Bad News*, London, Routledge & Kegan Paul.
Glasgow University Media Group (1982), *Really Bad News*, London, Writers & Readers.
Glennerster, H. (ed.) (1983), *The Future of the Welfare State*, London, Heinemann.
Golding, P. (1983), 'Rethinking commonsense about social policy', in Bull, D. and Wilding, P. (eds), *Thatcherism and the Poor*, London, Child Poverty Action Group.
Golding, P. and Middleton, S. (1978), *Images of Welfare* (mimeo), research report to Nuffield Foundation, London.

Golding, P. and Middleton, S. (1982), *Images of Welfare*, Oxford, Martin Robertson.

Goldmann, L. (1970), *Marxisme et sciences humaines*, Paris, Gallimard.

Goldmann, L. (1973), *The Human Sciences and Philosophy*, London, Cape.

Goodin, R. (1982), 'Freedom and the welfare state: theoretical foundations', *Journal of Social Policy*, vol. 11, no. 2.

Gough, I. (1979), *The Political Economy of the Welfare State*, London, Macmillan.

Gough, I. (1980), 'Thatcherism and the welfare state', *Marxism Today*, May 1980.

Gough, I. (1982), 'The crisis of the British welfare state', in Fainstein, S. and N. (eds), *Urban Policy Under Capitalism*, New York, Sage.

Gould, J. (1969), *Contemporary Political Thought*, London, Holt, Rhinehart & Winston.

Gould, F. and Roweth, B. (1980), 'Public spending and social policy: the United Kingdom, 1950–77', *Journal of Social Policy*, vol. 9, no. 3.

Gouldner, A. (1980), *The Two Marxisms*, London, Macmillan.

Government Actuary (1981), *Sixth Survey of Occupational Pension Schemes*, London, HMSO.

Griffith, J. (ed.) (1983), *Socialism in a Cold Climate*, London, Allen & Unwin.

Habermas, J. (1975), *Legitimation Crisis*, London, Heinemann.

Habermas, J. (1976), 'Legitimation Problems in Late Capitalism', in Connerton, P. (ed.), *Critical Sociology*, Harmondsworth, Penguin.

Hadley, R. and Hatch, S. (1981), *Social Welfare and the Failure of the State*, London, Allen & Unwin.

Hall, P., Land, H., Parker, R. and Webb, A. (1975), *Change, Choice and Conflict in Social Policy*, London, Heinemann.

Hall, S. (1971), *Deviancy, Politics and the Media* (mimeo), Birmingham University, Centre for Contemporary Cultural Studies.

Hall, S. (1972), *External Influences on Broadcasting* (mimeo), Birmingham University, Centre for Contemporary Cultural Studies.

Hall, S. (1973), *Encoding and Decoding in the Television Discourse* (mimeo), Birmingham University, Centre for Contemporary Cultural Studies.

Hall, S. (1977), 'The hinterland of science', in Birmingham University, Centre for Contemporary Cultural Studies, *On Ideology*, London, Hutchinson.

Hall, S. (1979), 'The great moving right show', *Marxism Today*, January 1979.

Hall, S. et al. (1978), *Policing the Crisis*, London, Macmillan.

Halsey, A., Heath, A. and Ridge, J. (1980), *Origins and Destinations*, London, Oxford University Press.

Harris, R. and Seldon, A. (1979), *Over-ruled on Welfare*, London, Institute of Economic Affairs.

Harrison, J. (1979), *The British Economic Disaster*, London, Pluto Press.

Hayek, F. (1972, 1976 and 1979), *Law Legislation and Liberty* (3 vols), London, Routledge & Kegan Paul.

Hill, M. (1980), *Understanding Social Policy*, Oxford, Blackwell.

Hirsch, F. (1977), *The Social Limits to Growth*, London, Routledge & Kegan Paul.

Hirsch, F. (1978), 'The State Apparatus and Social Reproduction', in Holloway and Picciotto, *op. cit.*

Hirst, P. (1976), 'Althusser and the theory of ideology', *Economy and Society*, vol. 5 no. 4.

Hirst, P. (1979), *On Law and Ideology*, London, Macmillan.

Hirst, P. and Woolley, P. (1982), *Social Relations and Human Attributes*, London, Tavistock.

HMSO (1954), *Report of the Committee on the Economic and Financial Problems for the Provision for Old Age* (Phillips Report), Cmd 9333, London, HMSO.

HMSO (1956), *Report of the Committee of Enquiry into the Cost of the NHS*

References

(Guillebaud Report), Cmd 9663, London, HMSO.

HMSO (1972), *Proposals for a Tax Credit Scheme*, Cmnd 5116, London, HMSO.

HMSO (1979), *The Government's Expenditure Plans, 1979–80 to 1981–82*, Cmnd 7746, London, HMSO.

HMSO (1980), *The Government's Expenditure Plans, 1980–81 to 1983–84*, Cmnd 7841, London, HMSO.

HMSO (1983), *The Government's Expenditure Plans, 1982–83 to 1984–85*, Cmnd 8494, London, HMSO.

Hobbes, T. (1968), *Leviathan*, Harmondsworth, Penguin.

Hobsbawm, E. (1972), 'Karl Marx's contribution to historiography', in Blackburn, R. (ed.), *Ideology in Social Sciences*, Harmondsworth, Penguin.

Hockley, G. and Harbour, S. (1982), 'Preferences for tax and spending', *Public Money*, March 1982.

Holloway, J. and Picciotto, S. (1978), *State and Capital*, London, Edward Arnold.

Humphries, J. (1977), 'Class struggle and the persistence of the working class family', *Cambridge Journal of Economics*, vol. 2, no. 3.

Hunt, A. (1970), *The Home Help Service in England and Wales*, London, HMSO.

Hunt, A. (1978), *The Elderly at Home*, London, HMSO.

Independent Schools Information Service (1983), *Independent Schools Statistics – 1983* (mimeo), London, Independent Schools Information Service.

Inland Revenue (1983), *The Cost of Tax Reliefs for Pension Schemes: The Appropriate Statistical Approach* (mimeo), London, Board of the Inland Revenue.

Jones, K., Brown, R. and Bradshaw, J. (1979), *Issues in Social Policy*, London, Routledge & Kegan Paul.

Jordan, W. (1976), *Freedom and the Welfare State*, London, Routledge & Kegan Paul.

Judge, K. (1981), 'State pensions and the growth of social welfare expenditure', *Journal of Social Policy*, vol. 10, no. 4.

Judge, K. (1982), 'The growth and decline of public spending', in Walker (1982), *op. cit.*

Judge, K. and Hampson, R. (1980), 'Political advertising and the growth of social welfare expenditure', *International Journal of Social Economics*, no. 7, no. 2.

Judge, K., Smith, J. and Taylor-Gooby, P. (1983), 'Public opinion and the privatisation of welfare', *Journal of Social Policy*, vol. 12, no. 4.

Kahn, S. and Kamerman, A. (eds) (1978), *Family Policy*, New York, Columbia University Press.

Karn, V. (1981), 'Housing allocation policies in Birmingham', paper presented to Civil Service College seminars on social policy.

Kavanagh, D. (1983), *Political Science and Political Behaviour*, London, Allen & Unwin.

Kent County Council (1978), *Education Vouchers in Kent*, Maidstone, Kent County Council.

Kincaid, J. (1975), *Poverty and Inequality in Britain*, Harmondsworth, Penguin.

Kincaid, J. (1978), 'The politics of pensions', *New Society*, 16 February 1978.

Klein, R. (1974), 'The case for elitism', *Political Quarterly*, vol. 45, no. 3.

Klein, R. (1976), 'The politics of public expenditure', *British Journal of Political Science*, vol. 6, no. 4.

Klein, R. (1980a), 'The welfare state: a self-inflicted crisis?' *Political Quarterly*, vol. 51, no. 4.

Klein, R. (1980b), 'The crisis in the welfare state?' paper delivered to Social Administration Association Conference, University of Leeds, 1980.

Land, H. (1976), 'Women: supporters or supported?' in Leonard, D. and Allen, S. (eds), *Sexual Divisions in Society*, London, Tavistock.

Land, H. (1978), 'Who cares for the family?' *Journal of Social Policy*, vol. 7, no. 3.

Land, H. and Parker, R. (1978), 'Family policy in Britain', in Kahn and Kamerman, *op. cit.*

Larrain, J. (1979), *The Concept of Ideology*, London, Hutchinson.

Layard, R., Metcalfe, D. and Nickell, S. (1979), 'The effect of collective bargaining in relative and absolute wages', *British Journal of Industrial Relations*, vol. 16, no. 3.

Le Grand, J. (1982), *The Strategy of Equality*, London, Allen & Unwin.

Leibenstein, H. (1965), 'Long-run welfare criteria', in Margolis, J. (ed.), *The Public Economy of Urban Communities*, Baltimore, Johns Hopkins.

Lenin, V. (1965), *The State and Revolution*, Peking, Foreign Language Press.

Leonard, P. (1979), 'Restructuring the welfare state', *Marxism Today*, December 1979.

Lewis, A. (1980), 'Attitudes to public expenditure', *Political Studies*, vol. 29, no. 2.

Lewis, J. (1983), 'Conceptualising equality for women', in Griffith (ed.), *op. cit.*

Lipsey, D. (1979), 'The reforms people want', *New Society*, 4 October 1979.

Locke, M. (1974), *Power and Politics in the School System*, London, Routledge & Kegan Paul.

Lukács, G. (1971), *History and Class Consciousness* (2nd edition), London, Merlin.

Lukes, S. (1976), 'Socialism and inequality', in Blowers, A. and Thompson, G. (eds), *Inequalities, Conflict and Change*, Milton Keynes, Open University Press.

Macafee, A. (1981), 'A glimpse of the black economy in official statistics', *Economic Trends*, May 1981.

MacGregor, S. (1981), *The Politics of Poverty*, London, Longman.

Machiavelli, N. (1970), *Discourses* (Crick, B., ed.), Harmondsworth, Penguin.

McIntosh, M. (1978), 'The State and the oppression of women', in Kuhn, A. and Wolpe, A. (eds), *Feminism and Materialism*, London, Routledge & Kegan Paul.

McIntosh, M. (1979), 'The Welfare State and the needs of the dependent family', in Burman, S. (ed.), *Fit Work for Women*, London, Croom Helm.

McIntosh, M. (1981), 'Feminism and social policy', *Critical Social Policy*, vol. 1, no. 1.

Maclure, J. (ed.) (1973), *Educational Documents*, London, Chapman & Hall.

MacPherson, C. (1968), 'Elegant tombstones', *Canadian Journal of Political Science*, vol. 1, no. 1.

McRobbie, A. (1974), *The Culture of Teenage Girls* (mimeo), Birmingham University, Centre for Contemporary Cultural Studies.

McRobbie, A. (1978), 'Working class girls and the culture of femininity', in Birmingham University, Centre for Contemporary Cultural Studies: *Women Take Issue*, London, Hutchinson.

Mannheim, K. (1936), *Ideology and Utopia*, London, Routledge & Kegan Paul.

Mannheim, K. (1968), *Essays on the Sociology of Knowledge*, London, Routledge & Kegan Paul.

Marcuse, H. (1956), *Eros and Civilisation*, London, Routledge & Kegan Paul.

Marx, K. (1859), *Preface to a Critique of Political Economy*, reprinted in Marx (1959), *op. cit.*

Marx, K. (1959), 'Preface to a critique of political economy', in Feuer, L. (ed.), *Marx and Engels: Basic Writings*, London, Fontana.

Marx, K. (1974), *Capital: Vol. I*, London, Lawrence & Wishart.

Marx, K. (1975), *Early Writings* (Coletti, ed.), Harmondsworth, Penguin.

Marx, K. and Engels, F. (1970), *The German Ideology*, London, Lawrence & Wishart.

Mattelard, A. (ed.) (1979), *Communication and Class Struggle*, vol. 1, New York, International General.

References

Metcalfe, D. (1982), 'Employment and Unemployment', in Prest, A. and Coppock, D. (1982), *The British Economy: A Manual of Applied Economics*, London, Weidenfeld & Nicolson.

Middlemas, K. (1979), *Politics in Industrial Society*, London, Andre Deutsch.

Miliband, R. (1973), *The State in Capitalist Society*, London, Quartet.

Miliband, R. (1974), 'Power and poverty', in Wedderburn, D. (ed.), *Poverty, Inequality and Class Structure*, Cambridge, Cambridge University Press.

Miliband, R. (1978), *Marxism and Politics*, London, Oxford University Press.

Miliband, R. (1982), *Capitalist Democracy in Britain*, Oxford, Oxford Unviersity Press.

Millett, K. (1971), *Sexual Politics*, London, Sphere.

Ministry of Health (1963), *Health and Welfare*, Cmnd 1973, London, HMSO.

Ministry of Pensions and National Insurance (1966), *The Financial and Other Circumstances of Retirement Pensioners*, London, HMSO.

Mishra, R. (1984), *The Welfare State in Crisis*, London, Wheatsheaf.

Muecke, D. (1972), *Irony*, London, Methuen.

Mueller, D. (1979), *Public Choice*, Cambridge, Cambridge University Press.

Murie, A. (1981), 'Council house sales', *New Society*, 19 November 1981.

Navarro, V. (1980), *Class Struggle, the State and Medicine*, London, Martin Robertson.

Neave, G. (1975), *How They Fared*, London, Routledge & Kegan Paul.

NHS Unlimited (1983), *The Conservatives, the NHS and Private Medicine* (mimeo), London, Frank Dobson, MP.

Nicholson, J. (1974), 'The distribution and redistribution of income in the United Kingdom', in Wedderburn, D. (ed.), *Poverty, Inequality and Class Structure*, Cambridge, Cambridge University Press.

Nicholson, J. and Brittan, A. (1979), 'The redistribution of income', in Atkinson, A. (ed.), *The Personal Distribution of Incomes*, London, Allen & Unwin.

Niskanen, W. (1971), *Bureaucracy and Representative Government*, Chicago, Aldine-Atherton.

Nissel, M. (1978), *Taxes and Benefits: Does Redistribution Help the Family?* London, Policy Studies Institute.

Norris, M. (1978), 'Those we like to help', *New Society*, vol. 45, no. 822, 6 July 1978.

Nozick, R. (1971), *Anarchy, State and Utopia*, Oxford, Blackwell.

Oakley, A. (1981), *Subject: Women*, London, Fontana.

O'Connor, J. (1973), *The Fiscal Crisis of the State*, New York, St James' Press.

OECD (1984), 'Social expenditure: erosion or evolution?' *OECD, Observer*, January 1984, pp. 2–6.

Offe, C. (1974), 'Structural problems of the Capitalist State', in, von Beyme, K. (ed.), *German Political Studies*, vol. 1, 1974, New York, Sage.

Offe, C. (1976), *Industry and Inequality*, London, Edward Arnold.

O'Higgins, M. (1981), 'Tax evasion and the self-employed', *British Tax Review*, 1981, no. 6.

O'Higgins, M. (1983), 'Rolling back the Welfare State', in Jones, C. and Stevenson, J. (eds), *Year-Book of Social Policy, 1982*, London, Routledge & Kegan Paul.

OPCS (1980), *The General Household Survey, 1978*, London, HMSO.

OPCS (1984), *The General Household Survey, 1981*, London, HMSO.

Pahl, J. (1980), 'Patterns of money management within marriage', *Journal of Social Policy*, vol. 9, no. 3.

Pahl, R. (1984), 'Household work strategies in economic recession', in Redclift, N. and Mingione, E. *Beyond Employment: Household Gender and Subsistence*, Oxford, Blackwell.

Piachaud, D. (1981), 'Peter Townsend and the Holy Grail', *New Society*, vol. 57, 1981, pp. 419–21.

Pinker, R. (1971), *Social Theory and Social Policy*, London, Heinemann.

Pinker, R. (1979), *The Idea of Welfare*, London, Heinemann.

Plamenatz, J. (1963), *Man and Society, Vol. II*, London, Allen & Unwin.

Plamenatz, J. (1975), *Karl Marx's Philosophy of Man*, Oxford, Clarendon Press.

Plant, R. (1980), 'Needs and welfare', in Timms, N. (ed.), *Social Welfare*, London, Routledge & Kegan Paul.

Pond, C. (1982), 'Taxation and Public Expenditure', in Walker (ed.) (1982), *op. cit.*, pp. 49–69.

Popper, K. (1972), *Conjectures and Refutations*, London, Routledge & Kegan Paul.

Powell, J. and Macleod, I. (1952), *The Social Services – Needs and Means*, London, Bow Group.

Prest, A. and Coppock, D. (1982), *The British Economy*, London, Weidenfeld & Nicolson.

Raphael, D. (1970), *Problems of Political Philosophy*, London, Macmillan.

Rawls, J. (1972), *A Theory of Justice*, London, Oxford University Press.

Reid, I. (1977), *Social Class Differences in Britain*, London, Open Books.

Reid, I. and Wormald, E. (1982), *Sex Differences in Britain*, London, Grant McIntyre.

Rein, M. (1976), *Social Science and Public Policy*, Harmondsworth, Penguin.

Riker, W. (1982), *Liberalism Against Populism*, New York, W. H. Freeman.

Ritchie, J. (1983), *Paying for Equalisation*, Manchester, Equal Opportunities Commission.

Roof (1983), 'Notes on shorthold', *Roof*, Shelter, London, January 1983, p. 6.

Room, G. (1979), *The Sociology of Welfare*, Oxford, Blackwell.

Rose, H. (1981), 'Rereading Titmuss: the sexual division of welfare', *Journal of Social Policy*, vol. 10, no. 4.

Rose, H. and Rose, S. (1982), 'Moving right out of welfare – and the way back', *Critical Social Policy*, vol. 2, no. 1.

Rose, R. (ed.) (1980), *Challenge to Governance*, New York, Sage.

Rose, R. (1983), *Getting By in the Three Economies*, Glasgow, Centre for the Study of Public Policy, Paper no. 110.

Rose, R. and Peters, S. (1978), *Can Government Go Bankrupt?* New York, Basic Books.

Royal Commission on the Distribution of Income and Wealth (1979a), *Report No. 7*, Cmnd 7595, London, HMSO.

Royal Commission on the Distribution of Income and Wealth (1979b), *Report No. 8*, Cmnd 7679, London, HMSO.

Royal Commission on the NHS (1979), *Report*, Cmnd 7615, London, HMSO.

Runciman, W. (1972), *Relative Deprivation and Social Justice*, Harmondsworth, Penguin.

Russell, B. (1961), *A History of Western Philosophy*, London, Allen & Unwin.

Rutter, M., Maughan, B., Mortimore, P. and Ouston, J. (1979), *Fifteen Thousand Hours*, London, Open Books.

Sarlvik, B. and Crewe, I. (1974), 'Partnership and policy choice', *British Journal of Political Science*, vol. 6, no. 2, pp. 273–90.

Sarlvik, B. and Crewe, I. (1983), *Decade of Dealignment*, Cambridge University Press.

Saville, J. (1975), 'The Welfare State: an historical approach', in Butterworth, E. and Holman, R. (eds), *Social Welfare in Modern Britain*, London, Fontana.

Sayers, J. (1982), *Biological Politics*, London, Tavistock.

Schlackman Organisation (1978), 'Report on research on public attitudes towards the supplementary benefits scheme' (mimeo), submitted to Central Office of Information, London.

Schumpeter, J. (1961), *Capitalism, Socialism and Democracy*, London, Routledge & Kegan Paul.

Seldon, A. (1977), *Charge!* London, Temple-Smith.

Seldon, A. (1981), *Wither the Welfare State*, London, Institute of Economic Affairs.

Sinfield, A. (1978), 'Analyses in the social division of welfare', *Journal of Social Policy*, vol. 7, no. 2.

Sinfield, A. (1981), *What Unemployment Means*, Oxford, Martin Robertson.

Sleeman, J. (1979), *Resources for the Welfare State*, London, Longman.

Social Security Advisory Committee (1983), *Second Report*, London, HMSO.

Steedman, J. (1980), *Progress in Secondary Schools*, London, National Children's Bureau.

Study Commission on the Family (1983), *Families in the Future*, London.

Taylor-Gooby, P. (1982), 'Two Cheers for the Welfare State', *Journal of Public Policy*, vol. 2, no. 4.

Taylor-Gooby, P. and Dale, J. (1981), *Social Theory and Social Welfare*, London, Edward Arnold.

Thane, P. (1982), *The Foundations of the Welfare State*, London, Longman.

Thatcher, M. (1979), 'Introduction' in *The Election Manifesto*, London, Conservative Central Party, p. 1.

Therborn, G. (1980), *The Ideology of Power and the Power of Ideology*, London, New Left Books.

Titmuss, R. (1955), 'The social division of welfare', in *Essays on the Welfare State*, London, Allen & Unwin.

Titmuss, R. (1962), *Income Distribution and Social Change*, London, Allen & Unwin.

Titmuss, R. (1974), *Social Policy*, London, Allen & Unwin.

Titmuss, R. (1976), *Essays on the Welfare State* (3rd edition), London, Allen & Unwin.

Townsend, P. (1965), *The Last Refuge*, London, Routledge & Kegan Paul.

Townsend, P. (1973), *The Social Minority*, Harmondsworth, Penguin.

Townsend, P. (1976), *Sociology and Social Policy*, London, Allen Lane.

Townsend, P. (1979), *Poverty in the United Kingdom*, Harmondsworth, Penguin.

Townsend, P. and Davidson, N. (1982), *Inequalities in Health*, Harmondsworth, Penguin.

Treasury, (1984), *The Next Ten Years: Public Expenditure and Taxation into the 1990s*, Cmnd 9189, London, HMSO.

Tullock, G. (1959), 'Some problems of majority voting', *Journal of Political Economics*, vol. 67, no. 4.

Tullock, G. (1976), 'Some problems of majority voting', in Arrow, K. and Scitovsky, T. (eds), *Readings in Welfare Economics*, Homewood, Illinois, Irwin.

Ungerson, C. (1982), *The Caring Capacity of the Community* (mimeo), research report to Social Science Research Council, London.

Walker, A. (ed.), (1982), *Public Expenditure and Social Policy*, London, Heinemann.

Walker, A. (1983), *Community Care*, London, Heinemann.

Weale, A. (1983), *Political Theory and Social Policy*, London, Macmillan.

West, P., Illsley, R. and Kelman, H. (1984), 'Public preferences for the care of dependency groups', *Social Science and Medicine*, vol. 18, no. 4.

Westergaard, J. and Resler, H. (1975), *Class in a Capitalist Society*, London, Heinemann.

Whiteley, P. (1981), 'Public opinion and the demand for welfare in Britain',
  Journal of Social Policy, vol. 10, no. 4.
Whiteley, P. and Winyard, S. (1983), 'Influencing social policy', *Journal of Social
  Policy*, vol. 12, no. 1.
Wilding, P. (1982), *Professional Power and Social Welfare*, London, Routledge &
  Kegan Paul.
Wilensky, H. (1976), *The New Corporation*, New York, Sage.
Willis, P. (1978), *Learing to Labour*, London, Saxon House.
Wilson, E. (1977), *Women and the Welfare State*, London, Tavistock.
Wolfe, A. (1979), *The Limits of Legitimacy*, New York, Macmillan.
Wolpe, A. (1978), 'Education and the division of labour', in Kuhn, A. and Wolpe,
  A. (eds), *Feminism and Materialism*, London, Routledge & Kegan Paul.
Wood, A. (1972), 'The Marxian critique of social justice', *Philosophy and Public
  Affairs*, Spring 1972.
Zweig, F. (1961), *The Worker in an Affluent Society*, London, Heinemann.

Subject index

Name Index